Books That Transport to Other Places

More Reviews of Books Too Good to Miss
With a Supplement for and About Kids

Donna DeLeo Bruno

Books that Transport to Other Places: More Reviews of Books Too Good to Miss
Copyright © 2017 Donna DeLeo Bruno. Produced and printed by Stillwater River Publications. All rights reserved. Written and produced in the United States of America. This book may not be reproduced or sold in any form without the expressed, written permission of the authors and publisher.

Visit our website at **www.StillwaterPress.com** for more information.

First Stillwater River Publications Edition

ISBN-10: 1-946-30018-7
ISBN-13: 978-1-946-30018-8

1 2 3 4 5 6 7 8 9 10
Written by Donna DeLeo Bruno
Published by Stillwater River Publications, Glocester, RI, USA.

The views and opinions expressed in this book are solely those of the author and do not necessarily reflect the views and opinions of the publisher.

Dedication

This book is dedicated with heartfelt appreciation to my grandmother, Ann Vona DiMezza, whose daily help with my children enabled me to continue, and continue, and continue my education through college, graduate school, and beyond.

TABLE OF CONTENTS

INTRODUCTION...i

LOCATIONS AROUND THE WORLD

THE TEA PLANTER'S WIFE *(Ceylon)* 1

THE LIGHT WE LOST *(New York City and the Middle East)* 3

THE ORPHAN KEEPER *(India)* 5

STATE OF WONDER *(Amazon Jungle)* 7

THE OTHER SIDE OF THE WORLD *(Australia)* 9

A FEW OF THE GIRLS *(Ireland)* 11

THE RENT COLLECTOR *(Cambodia)* 13

CROSSING THE BAMBOO BRIDGE *(Vietnam)* 15

HILLBILLY ELEGY *(Appalachia, Kentucky)* 17

EVERY MAN DIES ALONE *(Berlin, Germany)* 19

LILAC GIRLS *(Poland)* 21

KAROLINA'S TWINS *(Poland)* 23

MISCHLING *(Poland)* 25

THE BOY IN THE STRIPED PAJAMAS *(Poland)* 27

THE BOY AT THE TOP OF THE MOUNTAIN *(Germany)* 29

A PARIS AFFAIR *(France)* 31

LUNCHEON OF THE BOATING PARTY *(France)* 33

THE RAILWAYMAN'S WIFE *(Australia)* 35

VICTORIA *(England)* 37

CALL THE MIDWIFE -- Volume 2 *(England)* 39

BEHIND CLOSED DOORS *(England)* 43

ALL THE STARS IN THE HEAVENS *(Hollywood, California)* 45

IN THE PRESIDENT'S SECRET SERVICE *(Washiongton, D.C.)* 47

THE HOLLYWOOD DAUGHTER *(Hollywood, California)* 49

THE BOSTON GIRL *(Boston, Massachusetts)* 51

THE SISTERS OF HARDSCRABBLE BAY *(New Brunswick, Canada)* ...53

WELL-KNOWN PEOPLE

SETTLE FOR MORE 57

HANK 59

PORTRAITS OF COURAGE 61

A FRIEND OF MR. LINCOLN 63

THE GOOD SON 65

ROSEMARY 67

A LUCKY LIFE INTERRUPTED 69

THE CIVIL WARS OF JULIA WARD HOWE 71

BOYS IN THE TREES: A MEMOIR 73

SHIRLEY JACKSON 75

WINTER 77

MY WAY 79

A PIECE OF THE WORLD 81

FICTION and HISTORICAL FICTION

THE GILDED YEARS 85

LILLI DEJONG 87

GLORY OVER EVERYTHING 89

THE SUBMISSION 91

COMMONWEALTH 93

MISS JANE 95

THE WEDDING DRESS 97

MY NAME IS LUCY BARTON 99

ANYTHING IS POSSIBLE 101

EVENTIDE 103

THE DOLLHOUSE 105

THE DIARY 107

THE RUNAWAY WIFE 109

PRETENDING TO DANCE 111

WE NEVER ASKED FOR WINGS 113

THE CHILDREN'S CRUSADE	115
BASTARD OUT OF CAROLINA	117
THE SILVER STAR	119
THE HUSBAND'S SECRET	121
THE SECRET KEEPER	123
SAVE ME	125
SUMMER HOUSE WITH SWIMMING POOL	127
THE WRONG SIDE OF GOODBYE	129
BREAKING WILD	131
SOMEONE	133
ORPHAN # 8	135
A FIREPROOF HOME FOR THE BRIDE	137
HAPPY PEOPLE READ AND DRINK COFFEE	139
THE WOMAN UPSTAIRS	141
FAMILY PICTURES	143
SIRACUSA	145
A TREE GROWS IN BROOKLYN	147
IN THE SHADOW OF ALABAMA	149
THE LANGUAGE OF FLOWERS	151

NON-FICTION

LEGENDS OF THE WEST	155
SPINSTER	157
THE BLACK HAND	161
WHEN BOOKS WENT TO WAR	163
PROOF OF HEAVEN	167
AVIATRIX	169
THE MARRIAGE BUREAU	173

SUPPLEMENT: FOR AND ABOUT KIDS

GREAT BOOKS FOR KIDS	179
APPLEBLOSSOM THE POSSUM	183

FLORA & ULYSSES	185
TALES OF ZOFTIC	187
WHEN MISCHIEF CAME TO TOWN	189
ROLLER GIRL	191
THE LAND WITHOUT COLOR	193
CIRCUS MIRANDUS	195
WONDER	197
AL CAPONE DOES MY SHIRTS	199
COUNTING ON GRACE	201
THE WAR THAT SAVED MY LIFE	203
THE HIRED GIRL	205
FISH IN A TREE	207
FRIDAY BARNES	209
BOOKED	211
THE CHRISTMAS SWEATER	213
WOMEN IN SCIENCE	215
EVERYTHING, EVERYTHING	217
WAITING FOR JUNE	219
ANOTHER BROOKLYN	221
THE ABSOLUTELY TRUE DIARY OF A PART-TIME INDIAN	223
GRIT	225
QUIET	227
WHERE YOU GO IS NOT WHO YOU'LL BE	229
HOW CHILDREN SUCCEED	231
HOW TO TEACH YOUR CHILDREN SHAKESPEARE	233

INTRODUCTION

I am known as the "book-lady." For some years, I have written book reviews for the local newspapers which publish my picture with the reviews. Some of my readers stop me downtown as I do my errands at the post office, library, or supermarket and greet me with, "Oh, you're the 'book lady.' I enjoy your reviews. What are you reading now? What do you recommend?" Actually, I like being called the "book lady" since in my thirty-five years of high school teaching, I have been called a lot of things, some not too flattering when I found it necessary to discipline recalcitrant students intent on testing limits. I consider it a most apt epithet since, like Sinclair Lewis, "I can never find a cup of tea large enough or a book long enough to suit me." This has always been true as far back as I can remember. My fondest memories are of my mother reading me a bedtime story before sleep or curled up as a child in a window seat on a rainy day, completely "lost" in the pages of an absorbing story. My Aunt Rose, whom I remember with great fondness, lived with my Uncle Chuck on the second floor above my grandparents in a lovely three-floor stately Victorian house on lower High Street (Bristol, Rhode Island). On beautiful summer days when she felt that my sister and I were too long with our noses in a book, she would "throw us out" into the huge backyard to get some fresh air. But soon we would be clamoring at the locked door begging to be allowed to take our books outdoors with us. There was a gorgeous magnolia tree that blossomed so prolifically that my grandmother delighted in just gazing at it for hours when sitting by the kitchen window. My Uncle Chuck would complain each spring about the "mess" of petals it dropped, but what a great canopy of shade it provided for reading a good book. Sometimes Aunt Rose or my grandmother would relent, but usually we were encouraged to ride our bikes or take a walk downtown. Bristol, Rhode Island was a charming place when I was growing up in the '50s. It was a small "All American" town of many stately colonial homes, with well-maintained and well-manicured lawns and gardens on High Street. Some had never-ending, wrap-around porches bedecked with white rocking chairs on which every afternoon -- religiously around 3-4 PM, when their chores were complete -- the elderly owners would take their lemonades, or something stronger -- onto their porches to peruse the later newspaper -- in those days there were two editions -- the morning "Journal" and the evening "Bulletin." In our case, the Breens lived to the right of my grandparents and the Woods to the left. Further down were the Barlows and after them the Herreshoff sisters of the famous Nathaniel Herreshoff family, innovative and brilliant designers and builders of sailing yachts that won "The America's Cup." The water was everywhere, easily accessible at the end of nearly every street since Bristol is a peninsula surrounded by dazzling water on three sides. Most summer days, Aunt Rose would pack a picnic basket and together my sister and I, along with her and our three small cousins -- one usually in a large black perambulator popular in those days -- would hike around the corner to the "beach" at the foot of Union St. or Burton St. We would spread our blanket and while away the afternoon swimming, clamming, frolicking in the water, and, of course, reading when it was time to towel off and dry ourselves in the sun. Those were delightful times I remember with fond nostalgia. So books were part of my everyday activities, whether inside or out. My mother fostered and nourished my love of reading, providing me with wonderful reading material, particularly the classics. On our many bookshelves would be leather-bound copies of *Treasure Island, Moby Dick, A Tale of Two Cities, The Hunchback of Notre Dame, The Three Musketeers, The Man in the Iron Mask, Alice in Wonderland, Robinson Crusoe, etc.* -- a plethora of "riches." In addition, my sister and I would walk downtown to Rogers Free Library -- the original still there after these many years, although with a new wing -- and "stock up" on more reading material if -- God forbid -- we ran out. And so I guess I was a "book girl" long before I became the "book lady." My boys were avid readers growing up, my younger son very upset when he would loan a paperback to a friend and have it returned dog-eared with the front cover wrinkled from having been folded over the back. When he would bring home the order form for leisure books ordered through the Rockwell Elementary School he attended, he would check off nearly every one; and I would have to explain that that was why we had libraries, to "borrow" books rather than having to

Books that Transport to Other Places

buy them all. But he would be insistent that he wanted his "own" books to read again and again. So "the apple doesn't fall far from the tree," and now I am delighted to take recommendations from my grandchildren for good books for kids. They never disappoint me and so you will find some of their suggestions here, and you too will not be disappointed: *Al Capone Does My Shirts, Wonder, Roller Girl, Flora and Ulysses* are only a few of those they have suggested. So I hope that you and your children or grandchildren will enjoy both the adult titles and those savored by my own grandkids. I have culled a wide selection so that every single book reviewed within is a worthwhile read. Hoping you remain "booked" for hours of enduring pleasure!

Note: Please regard loosely the recommended ages for the books in the section "For and About Kids" since some children are precocious, mature, and well able to handle reading levels and subject matter far beyond their years. However, with such books as *The Boy in the Striped Pajamas* and *The Boy at the Top of the Mountain*, both of which deal with "The Holocaust," the stories are so heart-rending as to require an emotional ability to comprehend such serious historical events.

LOCATIONS AROUND THE WORLD

THE TEA PLANTER'S WIFE

by
Dinah Jefferies

Exotic and mysterious, *The Tea Planter's Wife,* is set in Ceylon when it was a British colony in the 1920s -- '30s. Gwendolyn Hooper has become the new bride of wealthy plantation owner Laurence Hooper with whom she had a whirlwind romance in England. What she doesn't realize is that with this union she has inherited a sister-in-law Verity who will live with them in Ceylon and whom her husband supports financially and emotionally. The sibling relationship is unusual since Verity seems to resent Gwen and is jealous of the time her brother spends with his wife. She appears to be in competition with Gwen for Laurence's attention. Also troubling is the fact that in the undergrowth surrounding the house, Gwen discovers a small tombstone which turns out to be that of Laurence's child with his first wife who is deceased. Of further intrigue is the native *Sinhalese* Savi Ravasinghe whom she met on her voyage and who seems always to hover on the periphery. Disliked but tolerated by Laurence, the swarthy Ravasinghe is a disturbing presence. In fact, it will be this unctuous figure who appears to wreak havoc in all their lives; but in this novel, things are never as they seem. Gwen tries her best to adapt to the new and strange environment, but there is so much with which to contend: a language she does not speak nor understand; the presence of an American businesswoman Christina, who is her husband's admiring business partner; the native Tamil and Hindu *appus, dhobis,* and ever-present housekeeper Navvena who seems aware of things unknown to Gwen; the alien setting with its oppressive heat and humidity, tree snakes, grass snakes, biting ants and beetles, wild boars, swamps, jungle inhabitants; the brusque overseer MacGregor with whom she shares an uneasy relationship. All this begins to take its physical and emotional toll on Gwen just as she becomes pregnant with twins. The birth will complicate all these various relationships and will comprise the rest of this story.

    This is an exceptionally good read, richly atmospheric and seductive. The author is adept at creating an aura of suspense which is sustained and heightened throughout. Secrets are gradually revealed and you want to keep feverishly reading to learn the outcome. A remarkable biological anomaly will provide answers to the mystery. Also mesmerizing is a sense of danger and a feeling that someone is plotting Gwen's demise. She too senses this as she is given a series of medicinal potions after childbirth to calm her nerves, lift her depression, and encourage her recovery, which instead seem to narcotize her. Soon she is craving their hypnotic effects. Read to find out if Gwen survives intact the many overwhelming personal, physical, and psychological challenges that are working to unravel her and her marriage. This is one I recommend highly.

THE LIGHT WE LOST

by
Jill Santopolo

Two college students, Lucy and Gabe, meet in a Shakespeare seminar at Columbia University and share an experience on 9/11 that will forever bind them together. From the rooftop of Gabe's dorm, both will witness with horror and disbelief the attack on the Twin Towers in Manhattan. This day will begin an intense and emotionally powerful relationship that will endure a lifetime. In the first phase, they are completely intoxicated with each other, delighting in every new aspect of their lives together. They share idealistic hopes and dreams; Lucy of becoming a producer/director of children's TV shows, and Gabe a photojournalist traveling the world with his camera to capture the world's problems in need of address. In their work, they hope to make a positive impact on society and the future. But their goals will separate them since Gabe will indeed become a successful photographer known worldwide while Lucy will put her effort and talent into creating "It Takes a Galaxy" which will win awards. Although they are together as a couple only 14 months, that period will be remembered as the best of their lives. The sheer joy and exhilaration of this time will never be duplicated. The "light" will never again shine as brightly for either – hence the title. Lucy is so consumed by her love for Gabe that when he leaves for the Middle East, she is in despair -- devastated, heartbroken, unable to function. Try as she might, she cannot get over the loss. Eventually she will marry and become a mother, but she will forever compare her bliss with Gabe to the more moderate tone of her marriage. There is a great degree of conflict here -- among the various characters -- Lucy, her husband, and Gabe -- as well as personal struggles. Both she and Gabe will remain in distant touch through his occasional emails from battle-torn countries and even very brief encounters when he is in New York for a day or two on business. But what makes this love story different from other romance novels is the intensity and life-altering emotions that remain with both throughout their lifetimes. The impact that they have had on each other is embedded in their bodies and psyches forever, and the author writes with a poetic quality that enhances their special bond. There are some bittersweet as well as tragic surprises at the end which I must say I predicted halfway through the book. Nevertheless, it captures so well the fact that the early and formative experiences of our youth, both positive and negative, are probably the rawest and most keenly felt than at any other age.

THE ORPHAN KEEPER

by
Camron Wright

Based on a true story and actual events, *The Orphan Keeper* is the sad tale of the 1978 kidnapping of a 7-year-old boy named Chellamuthu from his home in a slum in Erode, India.

Although raised in dire poverty with an irresponsible, alcoholic father who once burned his feet with coals for disobedience, the boy is loved by his mother, brothers, sisters, and extended family.

One day while standing outside a building in town where his father, who has an errand, has instructed him to remain, a van pulls up, forces him inside, and ferries him to an unknown destination, the Lincoln Home for Homeless Children. In this walled compound, he observes other children -- mostly babies -- being fed and bathed. He attempts to convey to Eli, the man in charge, that he has a family and does not belong here, but is unsuccessful. In the months he is imprisoned here, he takes to caring for a very ill baby girl named Anu who is wasting away. With her he forms a bond and a purpose for living since he remains with her day and night squeezing drops of water into her mouth, keeping her hydrated as she is plagued by vomiting and diarrhea. His misery is compounded when Eli tells him that his father sold him, since he has been yearning for his family, totally heartbroken at their separation. Unable to cope with his grief, he feels certain his heart is going to rupture. Confusion, disillusionment, anger, and depression overwhelm him, and the reader shares his pain and suffering. At one point, Chellamuthu attempts a harrowing escape through a sewage pipe, where he squeezes like a rat, covered in feces, urine, and waste, suffocated by putrid odors, just too horrible to imagine. Once outside the gates, he is covered with scrapes and cuts, bleeding profusely, unable to escape the stench that contaminates him.

But eventually he returns, because his conscience will not allow him to forsake Anu to her certain death.

But Eli tells the boy that in his absence Anu has been sent to America for adoption; and losing his tether to his homeland entirely, the stricken child feels forsaken and adrift. Eventually he will be adopted by an American couple, Fred and Linda, given a new name Taj, and enrolled in a US school where he is an anomaly—unable to communicate, the only black in his entire town. Even one of his younger step-brothers (also an adoptee) refuses to touch him for fear that he "too will turn black!" It is extreme culture shock to be sure; and the last straw comes, when Linda unknowingly washes his bed sheets under which he had hidden a drawing of his family made when he was still able to picture them. The accumulation of sorrow and anger explode, but Linda is determined to nurture this damaged child. Eventually when she learns that he has a mother and family in India, she will help him reunite. However, his early suffering and feelings of mistrust and betrayal will carry into his adulthood, leaving him forever scarred.

There is so much tension and inner conflict which the author skillfully conveys as to make the reader want to sweep in and rescue the child. We are deeply moved by his pain and loss, emotionally riveted by his predicament. What is ironic is that at age 18, he is placed with an authentic Indian host family during a school semester abroad in London, where he is dismayed at their eating habits (hands instead of utensils); the noisy, crowded atmosphere of their flat; their strange food and alien language. HE IS AMERICAN!!! Who ARE these unusual, foreign people?

The Orphan Keeper is one good read with great moments of drama in which one is drawn into the character's mind and heart. It is an achingly tender portrait of a child bereft of all with whom he was familiar, plagued by a sense of betrayal and loss of trust in human relationships. Camron Wright is also the renowned author of *Letters for Emily*, a Readers' Choice Award Winner which was published in Japan, Australia, New Zealand, Germany, Korea, the Netherlands, and China, in addition to the US.

STATE OF WONDER

by
Ann Patchett

Exotic! Mysterious! Compelling! Brilliantly unusual! All these adjectives apply to *State of Wonder* which takes place in the Amazon jungle -- primitive, isolated, and far from civilization. A pharmaceutical company has sent researcher Dr. Swenson to Brazil to investigate a tribe whose females are able to have babies well into their 70s. Of course, if this is true, their scientists will be able to develop a cure for infertility reaping them astronomical financial profit. But Dr. Swenson is hidden somewhere deep in the wilderness and does not choose to communicate, although the company is funding her research. As a result, they send another researcher, Anders Eckman, to track her down and check on her progress. When Anders never returns, they send another, Maria Singh, into this "heart of darkness," an environment which resembles that of Joseph Conrad's classic novels. So begins an engrossing plot involving secrets, danger, suspense, and survival. Patchett is masterful in creating a magical but eerie setting -- an environment of maddening insects, lush but threatening foliage, unforgiving heat and moisture, snake-infested swamps -- even a feverish, paranoia-inducing atmosphere. Something in the air has a sort of hypnotizing effect that overwhelms all who dare to venture there. This is one, gripping, seductive tale in which Patchett masterfully weaves the parts of her narrative to keep you reading. Most surprising is the product that enables post-menopausal woman to conceive. This is one author with a fertile imagination and the writing talent to utilize it in the creation of one fantastical good read. Despite what might require a "willing suspension of disbelief," the reader is mesmerized by Patchett's skill in creating a believable story with captivating characters, particularly Dr. Swenson and Marina who have a past history from years ago when Dr. Swenson was Marina's professor/supervisor in the practice of obstetrics. Best of all, Patchett's vivid description captures the sounds, sights, and horrors of the jungle to create a forbidding place that often makes one cringe; but it is this frightening quality that keeps you reading. Moreover, is the ethical question regarding man's interference with the natural process of reproduction and procreation. A powerful book well-worth your time.

THE OTHER SIDE OF THE WORLD

by
Stephanie Bishop

In this truly outstanding novel, Henry, an Anglo-Indian, convinces his British wife Charlotte to relocate with him to Australia, which to her seems "the other side of the world."

Even from his first mention of this move, Charlotte is hesitant, reluctant to leave England where she feels an affinity for the landscape, their village, and home. Having lived abroad most of his life after birth in India, he has never developed a connection to a place and does not realize what he is asking his wife to give up. She is forlorn from the very moment of their arrival. While he is eager to begin a new job and raise their family in this remote place, Charlotte becomes more and more disillusioned and dismayed with all that seems foreign to her -- the oppressive heat, the unrelenting insects, the loneliness, and isolation. Overwhelmed with the demands of a toddler and an infant and with no outlet for her frustration, she begins to descend into hopelessness and despair. Henry, though he loves her dearly, is deaf to her pleas to return to England, even though all his attempts to cultivate their barren homestead fail miserably and repeatedly. In addition to his wife's unhappiness is the prejudice he encounters at his university position when he arrives. Having never interviewed him personally and assuming he was British, his academic superiors are surprised to find he is part Indian. But as his wife sinks further and further into depression, Henry is unable to admit that this endeavor has been a mistake. This is not only a portrait of a disintegrating marriage, but also a study of identity, of where one hails from, of childhood memories that root a person to a geographical area that affect one's way of viewing the world. Because Henry lacks this bearing, he cannot comprehend his wife's sense of dislocation and inability to adapt to this unfamiliar and foreign country. This is very much a psychological novel, including Charlotte's intense feelings of inadequacy as a nurturing mother. The author conveys in powerful language Charlotte's suffering and guilt when she fails to live up to her own expectations, feeling compelled to ignore and even abandon her children in order to maintain her sanity and individuality. She feels compelled to escape this barren wasteland, her insensitive husband, and her ever-clinging, ever-draining, ever-demanding babies. The author very skillfully builds the tension to the devastating climax of Charlotte's psychic unraveling. The reader suffers with her since she is so alone, desperate, and adrift in coping with her situation. "The Other Side of the World" is also extremely atmospheric as the author vividly details the settings of the English countryside –- the green foliage, the sea, the wind, the trees and gardens -- Charlotte relished in contrast to the oppressive Australia –- she abhors its aridness, lack of rain, unrelenting brown dust, bugs, rodents, and sweat. Bishop succeeds in making palpable Charlotte's deep sorrow, emptiness, and bewilderment at what she has become. It is not at all surprising that this book was listed for the Stella Prize 2016, the Indie Book Awards 2016, as well as the Australian/Vogel Literary Award and the Victorian Premier's Literary Award. Moreover, it won the Readings Prize for New Australian Fiction 2015 and the Australian Book Industry Award for Literary Fiction Book of the Year 2016. As a result, Bishop has been named one of the "Best Young Australian Novelists."

A FEW OF THE GIRLS

by
Maeve Binchy

In my earlier book *One Who Reads Is Always Booked* in which I reviewed Maeve Binchy's novel *Chestnut Street*, I indicated that it would be her last since she had just passed away in 2012. However, *A Few of the Girls* is a recently published collection of her short stories written over the decades. Like her twenty "Best-selling" novels, these stories are homespun vignettes of moments in the lives of very ordinary women, some at crossroads in their lives. For example, "A Result" is narrated in the first person ("I") who decides on the eve of her wedding not to marry, although she is two months pregnant. Keeping the news secret from everyone, including the father, she moves away to a new location, starts a new life, and raises the child alone. In "Love and Marriage," Cara, a writer, must decide whether she can leave the stimulating atmosphere of a city to marry her humble but loving boyfriend for a life in a quiet, country town. In some cases, the antagonist is not a husband or boyfriend, but a parent or relative. In "Falling Apart," Clare must negotiate how to deal with a controlling mother and make her own choices in order to lead her own life. "Forgiving" also involves a woman estranged from her family for more than 30 years because they opposed her choice of a husband long ago. Some of the characters undergo an "epiphany" of sorts as when Laura, in "No Tears in Tivoli," realizes that it is easy to stay married to her husband "as long as she lives by his rules." Similarly, Ronnie in "Catering for Love" is surprised to be told by her caterer that she recognizes Ronnie's "gentleman caller" as the same man she served at another woman's house the previous night. There are surprises here, as well as touches of irony as when a "friend" pretending to help a girl keep her man, steals him from right under her nose.

The author uses clever techniques, as in telling a story from the cat's point of view; in this case "Audrey," the pet, saves the day. In "The Custardy Case," the narrator is a 7-year-old boy who cannot understand the cause for the tension in his household, and no one will answer his questions about what's going on. Of course, it involves his placement in his parents' imminent divorce and he has misunderstood the term "custody."

Binchy's insight and skillful revelation of character is apparent in the stories dealing with female friendships: "Someone's Got to Tell Her," "Living Well," and "Chalk and Cheese." Other plots are told through the gossip of friends in a conversational, rambling style when the individual is not there to hear the appraisals of her. One tale is told entirely from listening to one end of a telephone conversation. And, as is typical of some females, despite the closeness -- or because of it --there is the inevitable comparisons about each's attractiveness, wealth, possessions, husbands, talents, etc.

Binchy knows women intimately; after all, she has spent a lifetime observing and writing about them: their desire for closeness, intimacy, competition, their romantic natures, fears of losing their husbands, blindness to unpleasantness they choose not to acknowledge, contention with parents and siblings. One story is about the obsessive need to be the ultimate hostess, superior to all in giving dinner parties. This is the stuff of women's lives -- for some it comprises all of their lives, and Maeve tells it all in simple, direct fashion. This is why she has remained so popular throughout her career. The women she portrays and the conflicts they encounter resonate with her female readers.

THE RENT COLLECTOR

by
Camron Wright

Sometimes it is enlightening to encounter a book set in a very different world from our own.

Such is the case with *The Rent Collector* which takes place in a waste dump in Cambodia where families live in make-shift lean-tos consisting of cardboard and tarps while earning a few pennies a day sifting through waste and garbage. It is daunting and dangerous work, scavenging for plastics and recyclables amid bacteria-laden junk and smoky air heavy with pollution. Not only is the heat unbearable, but heavy rubber boots must be worn to protect from flies, filth, vermin, smoldering fires, and sharp metals. It is here in poverty-stricken Phnom Penh, that Ki, his young wife Sang Ly, and their chronically ill baby Nisay struggle to survive one day at a time. In addition to the physical misery, is the danger of attack and robbery by other gangs of scavengers competing for their livelihood in the same manner, as well as constant demands by the intimidating, witchy, alcoholic rent collector known as Sopeap. But this shrew is much more than what she initially appears to be. In bits and pieces, her past will be revealed when she becomes a reading teacher to Sang Ly, who, despite her horrible, depressing surroundings, has an unquenchable thirst for knowledge. She is the most serious and attentive student, while Sopeap is the most demanding and difficult of instructors. The real mystery as to Sopeap's background arises when she introduces Sang Ly to literary greats and their masterpieces: *Moby Dick* by Melville, *Alice in Wonderland* by Lewis Carroll, *Pilgrim's Progress* by Paul Bunyan, *Kubla Khan* by Samuel Taylor Coleridge, writings by Swiss psychiatrist Carl Jung, works by Robert Louis Stevenson, John Steinbeck, William Shakespeare, etc. Where would this ragged, drunken hag, living in the most squalid of environments, have acquired such knowledge and a plethora of books? This is a most interesting story about the power of words and literature to not only instruct, but also to enable readers to transcend their boundaries and surroundings, as well as touch their hearts and souls. Much of what student and teacher peruse leads to deep questions about good and evil, the purpose of life, the meaning of dreams, the concept of hope, the essence of love, and life after death. Sang Ly is often frustrated, accusing the old woman of speaking in riddles, unable to decipher the meaning or symbolism of many of the stories; but the teacher will stoke her imagination and encourage patience in understanding. Not all stories have obvious, clear-cut themes and lessons, just as life does not proceed in a direct path, foreseeable future, or neat ending.

Read this very unusual, intriguing, intelligent portrayal of individuals living in such an uninhabitable place, but still able to find contentment and purpose -- and how kindness, love, generosity, and hope can survive amidst such squalor. Most intriguing, read to learn the traumatic experiences that transformed Sopeap's life and how she redeems herself.

CROSSING THE BAMBOO BRIDGE

by
Mai Donohue

Crossing the Bamboo Bridge is an inspiring true story of courage, determination, and resilience. Raised in poverty in a rural Vietnam hamlet, Mai was denied the education she so desired because in her culture it was believed that not only was learning unnecessary for a girl but also not conducive to becoming an obedient wife. Her father was killed by the local Viet Minh leaving her mother to raise the family; Mai, the victim of her mother's fear, anxiety, and angry tirades, was often beaten and scolded. While her brother and cousin were allowed to attend school, Mai had to be content with taking their schoolbooks secretly behind the house and using small sticks to copy the letters in an attempt to teach herself. At 14 she was forced to marry a much older man, ending her short childhood. But her iron will would not allow her to submit to the demands of a cruel, tyrannical, and abusive husband, as well as a repressive culture that dictated her proper role to be a subservient and passive wife. She fled a number of times before and after she became a mother, but she was always forced to return. Finally, in desperation, she made her escape to Saigon. This was not the end of her adversities, but rather a daily struggle to survive on the streets of an unfamiliar city. This book is a compelling and riveting tale of one female's valiant struggle to overcome oppression and find freedom and personal fulfillment. Although sorely tested at times, enduring one travail after another, Mai never allowed herself to be defeated. In her memoir, this courageous woman narrates her plight in frank, simple prose, all the more elegant for its truth and simplicity, maintaining her own voice throughout. A true heroine, Mai maintained her personal dignity in situations that would cower a weaker person. Her defiance, pride, and determination to better her lot will garner your respect. When subjected to inhumane treatment and told, "Accept your life; you are just a country girl

…foolish, dumb and stupid" she chose to rise above that assessment. This biography has all the ingredients of an excellent novel: an exotic setting, intense conflict, ever-rising suspense, and a REAL heroine, worthy of the reader's admiration. In addition, there are very touching scenes as when Mai peeks through the fence of the Officers' Club watching girls dancing in the arms of the men. Yearning to be held in such a protective embrace, she would wrap her arms around her small body, hugging herself as would a loving partner as "she danced alone in the dark." This will be a turning point because it is at this club that Mai will encounter the person who will change the course of her life.

HILLBILLY ELEGY
A Memoir of a Family and Culture in Crisis

by
J. D. Vance

One of the best books -- truly outstanding -- that I have read all year, *Hillbilly Elegy* left me wanting to shout "Bravo! Well done! Hooray!" For the author J. D. Vance's amazing escape from the poverty and dire hopelessness of Kentucky's Appalachia to a successful and happy life in Ohio living "The American Dream" was no small accomplishment. Born into a hard-drinkin,' hard-cussin,' hard livin,' hillbilly family, as dysfunctional as they come in one of the country's poorest areas, JD faced so many obstacles and personal challenges as to make his success truly remarkable. Told with naked honesty and a sobering realization of how his life might have turned out otherwise, the author himself marvels at his bright future despite all the odds that were stacked against him. His mother, although the salutatorian of her high school class, succumbed to hard drugs and alcohol early on, tying up with man after man each of whom became a series of temporary "dads" to her children on a revolving door basis. Before he and his sister Lindsay moved in with his "tough-as nails" grandparents, Mamaw and Papaw, they had transferred at the end of every school year to a different location and with each move came a new "boyfriend" -- Chip, Steve, Matt, Ken, Bob, etc. At the end of his ninth grade, JD even moved in with his mom's latest -- a stranger with three kids of his own. It was a daily struggle with the constant chaos surrounding him -- drunken, violent fights; breaking furniture; screaming insults; swearing, pulling, grabbing, pushing, and punching. When the chaos became too much, he and Lindsay would seek refuge with their grandparents. It was this source of unconditional affection and safety that allowed him to remain sane amidst all the turmoil and instability engulfing him. He describes this mess of domestic abuse and violence through the eyes of the confused and terrified child he was at the time, and evokes such sympathy that the reader yearns to run in to rescue and comfort him. Besides narrating the compelling crises that comprised his young life, J.D. cites many psychological studies focused on the after-effects of such trauma in childhood. Fortunately for him, he had powerful mentors in school who recognized and encouraged his potential. Still, his matriculation at the ultimately prestigious Yale Law School and later acceptance into a premier law firm were beyond his wildest expectations.

Read this deeply moving and frank evolution of one poor, country youngster. So absorbing that I completed it in 24 hours, I was so caught up not only in his own trials and tribulations, but those of his family and neighbors, fiercely proud and loyal survivors. This is a "colorful" cast of characters who live by their own unique set of values, somewhat like the Hatfield and the McCoy clans. What the author also addresses is the culture shock of having made it from such a crude, unsophisticated, and uneducated background to the posh atmosphere of elite mansions, restaurants, and even into the most exalted halls as an aide to a US Senator. He asserts that his experience in the US Marine Corps after high school and his stint in Iraq provided him with the self-confidence and direction he needed to set him on the path to achieving his dreams. It is to this branch of the military that he attributes the hard-earned lessons that served him well in his rise. Even after that, he had to face another learning curve regarding the proper attire for a job interview, the proper table etiquette with all those pieces of cutlery whose use he did not know, the advantages of networking, and all his social deficiencies which would be handicaps to his progress.

There is so much in this book even as he probes solutions to the plight of those tough unfortunates -- unschooled, unmentored, unconnected, and unemployed -- whom he has left behind in stagnant, rural Appalachia. He is acutely aware that for them upward mobility is presently unlikely; and he contemplates how to rescue and assist those like him who, with the proper programs and avenues to economic growth, might realize their inner potential. This is one excellent, frank assessment of his beloved, but flawed "hillbilly" family and neighbors and his escape from the quagmire that is their lives.

EVERY MAN DIES ALONE

by
Hans Fallada

A masterpiece based on a true story during WWII, *Every Man Dies Alone* is set in Nazi-occupied Berlin where an ordinary couple, Otto and Anna Quangel, make an irrevocable decision. They have just lost their beloved only son on the front, and they are not only broken-hearted but also bitter and angry at Hitler and his Third Reich whom they hold responsible for the terrible situation in Germany. Everyone is under suspicion; neighbors spy on neighbors; everyone is tense and fearful; food is scarce; beatings, arrests and torture are common even for innocent loyal citizens who have done nothing wrong. All exist in a state of high anxiety waiting for an ominous Gestapo knock on the door. Of course, most Germans are aware that Jews are being hauled off in large numbers to concentration camps. But Otto and Anna are hardworking, steadfastly decent German citizens who have never dabbled in politics; in fact, Otto, a master cabinet maker, is an extremely reticent loner who adeptly supervises a woodworking factory in near silence. Just a severe look at an unproductive worker is sufficient to get that person moving. At home he is the same, rarely speaking, content to live a quiet life with Anna, as unassuming as her husband. But the mutual loss of their son compels them to feel that they must DO something to thwart the despised Fuhrer and his Nazi war machine. An unobtrusive drudge with no other interest than work -- a man without a single friend -- Otto is the least likely individual one would expect to challenge anything. Nevertheless, Otto decides to write anti-war postcards which, with Anna's assistance, will be dropped in hallways and on windowsills in Berlin's public buildings. So begins an extremely dangerous, life-threatening enterprise in which they are risking both their lives. This is a compelling, highly suspenseful story, especially when one realizes the "Otto" and "Anna" were names for an actual couple who heroically resisted the Nazi regime of oppression. Their rebellion gave a noble and ethical purpose to their existence, sustaining their hope that these notes would be picked up by other German citizens whose sense of justice might be piqued so that they too might be encouraged to resist.

This is one great story of cat-and-mouse as an Inspector Escherich is assigned the mission of catching this "Hobgoblin," the epithet he gives the culprit. Tension mounts with unexpected twists in a masterful novel with the riveting sense of a compelling, utterly gripping thriller. Betrayal, appetite for vengeance, wartime adventure and high drama, an intricate plot set in turbulent times, psychological examination and emotionally astute perception of complicated characters -- all this and more make this a truly remarkable book. With the turn of each page, these characters -- Otto and Anna -- are caught up in a defiant scheme that becomes inevitably more and more dangerous. Falada's prose is superior and *Every Man Dies Alone* is a tremendous literary achievement!

LILAC GIRLS

by
Martha Hall Kelly

Lilac Girls by Martha Hall Kelly is a deeply affecting novel focused on four girls caught up in the Nazi Holocaust during WWII. Kasai Kusmerick, a Polish teenager, is about to find her world turned upside down following her involvement as a secret courier in the Polish Underground. Together with her older sister Zusannah, a medical student, and their mother Matka, she will be arrested and transported to Ravensbruck, Hitler's sole concentration camp for women. These two sisters are based on actual people. The other two main characters are Herta Oberheuser, a German female doctor who will set aside all human compassion and integrity to perform experimental surgery on these innocent and unsuspecting young Polish girls who are prisoners there. Dr. Oberheuser too was a real person hired by the most powerful men under Hitler's command, who later was tried with them at Nuremberg for crimes against humanity. Her operations consisted of inserting bacteria, wood, glass, and other contaminated material into perfectly healthy leg tissue which then was treated with an experimental substance to see its effect on the infection that would inevitably result. The surgery was brutal, unnecessary, life-threatening, and disfiguring since most of the subjects who survived were left with extremely damaged legs, referred to as "the rabbits" because they were left limping on crutches due to severely atrophied limbs. The fourth main character, New York socialite Caroline Ferriday, was in real life a tireless advocate and fund-raiser supporting the rehabilitation of this group of females after the war. The author adeptly weaves an intriguing plot from the horrendous and heartbreaking experiences of these actual women and the female physician who exploited them mercilessly to further her advancement with the Reich. The ending delves into the concept of post-traumatic stress syndrome, desire for revenge, atonement, justice, appropriate punishment for such evil on innocents, and ultimately forgiveness. An entirely gripping novel, *Lilac Girls* is remarkable for Martha Kelly's debut as a writer. She creates suspense while telling a gut-wrenching and compelling tale. Perhaps her characters seem so authentic because they were based on real persons. Generated throughout is an intense depth of feeling, as Kelly creates a jarring, searing story set amidst the cruel backdrop of turbulence and inhumanity in war-torn occupied Poland. The author so draws the reader into the piercing human drama of these well-delineated characters that I found the book "unput-downable."

KAROLINA'S TWINS

by
Ronald H. Balson

A promise made 70 years ago in Nazi-occupied Poland by one Jewish survivor to a friend is the crux of the historical novel *Karolina's Twins*. Lena Woodward has come to lawyer Catherine Lockhart and her investigator husband Liam for help in finding a set of Jewish twin infants abandoned in a field during the war in an attempt to save them from certain execution by the Gestapo. In her narration of her experiences as a prisoner of war, Lena describes to Catherine and Liam the darkest hours of her life, the execution of her parents and brother, the forced marches from one concentration camp to another, the unsanitary conditions of the Jewish ghettos where lice, typhus, malnutrition, lack of hygiene, and frigid cold took the lives of one friend after another. As an inmate at Birkenau with its gas chambers and crematoriums, she endured daily terror, as well as inhumane treatment and suffering. Now an elderly, wealthy widow, Lena has decided to exert every effort and expense to locate the twin sisters, but there are problems. First, her only son Arthur is challenging his mother's mental competency, insisting that this obsession with finding two children is a figment of her imagination, the onset of dementia. He is convinced that she is spending his inheritance on a futile search. In addition, there is no evidence that these children, if real, ever survived the Holocaust. As Lena describes the dangers lurking around every corner, the barbaric treatment by German officers, the furtive hiding and attempts to escape detection, the reader accompanies her on a heart-stopping, frantic struggle for survival. This is a compelling read full of twists and turns, suspense and surprise. One moment she is ruthlessly betrayed and the next rescued and saved by the most unlikely individuals. Interestingly enough, the character of Lena Schienman is based on a real woman named Fay who sought out the author to share her remarkable story. Like Lena in this novel, she was raised in Chrzanov and was forced to work sewing German uniforms in a shop overseen by an underground collaborator who enlisted her for espionage. In essence it is a true story confirmed by the author's extensive research at the Holocaust Museums in Washington and Skokie, as well as Yad Vashem in Jerusalem. From his study, Balsom is able to accurately portray the history of WW II Poland. The book is replete with historic dates and events, names of real people and places, so as to provide a lesson in history regarding the systematic efforts by the Third Reich to exterminate the Jewish population and those patriots who defied those efforts. These historic facts provide the background for an absorbing tale of the cruelest inhumanity of the 20th century. There is powerful and mounting tension in this emotionally riveting novel of loss, endurance, survival, and renewal.

MISCHLING

by
Affinity Konar

Mischling focuses on the heroic struggle for survival of a set of twins, Sasha and Pearl, in the face of overwhelming deprivation, agonizing suffering, and extreme adversity. Both become the victims of diabolical experimentation at the hands of Nazi Dr. Joseph Mengele, aka "The Angel of Death." At Auschwitz he performs sadistic experimental surgeries on multiples (twins, triplets, etc.) for his own "sick" genetic research. The perversions he wreaks on their bodies and psyches is heinous and barbaric. This is not a book for the faint-hearted as the author, in vivid, riveting, and heart-rending prose, captures and conveys the full horror of this particular concentration camp filled with pain, despair, and hopelessness. It is a terrifying world they inhabit -- the so-called children of "The Zoo" -- surrounded by the dead and dying and themselves caged like animals. Once they are selected as Mengele's "special children," who are ironically instructed to call him "Uncle," he will probe their bodies and minds, like lab specimens. One twin he will leave intact while the other will become his "guinea-pig" whose sight, hearing, and mobility will be destroyed. These "chosen" ones will be injected with germs, bacteria, viruses, and poisons; but what injures them most is his separation of siblings who share a similar nature in an attempt to strip them of their identity. Worse than the lice, hunger, fear, cold, brutality, and violence is their inconsolable grief at losing their other half, an eternal longing to reconcile this division of self. Each yearns for the "sameness" that was her sister and the ability to "read each other's thoughts" which has been destroyed. *Mischling* is one spell-binding tale -- harrowing, chilling, and haunting -- with a sort of supernatural quality of transcendence. It is a powerful story of longing, of the unbreakable bond between sisters who cannot survive wholly without each other.

Both suffer an agonizing sense of absence and incompleteness. After liberation by the Russians, Stasha, believing her sister dead, joins Feliks, another bereaved twin, in a joint effort to seek vengeance. Despite danger lurking everywhere, they make their trek to Warsaw in hopes of finding Mengele to seek justice for his crimes.

Despite the darkness of the subject matter, there is evidence of humanity in the form of other characters: Dr. Miri, a Jewish female physician forced to record Mengele's observations; her co-worker called "Twins' Father," a Polish infantryman also coerced to do Mengele's bidding; Bruna, an albino, herself subjected to study and inhumane experiments. Nevertheless, in and of itself, *Mischling* depicts the resilience and triumph of the human spirit, though broken, frayed, and nearly destroyed. If there is a message, it is that humanity can exist among desolation, cruelty, and inhumanity; and that the spirit can be resurrected and healed through love.

THE BOY IN THE STRIPED PAJAMAS

by
John Boyne

     How can an author write a book about The Holocaust without ever mentioning the specific horrors it generated? John Boyne has done just that by telling the experiences of nine- year-old Bruno, an innocent and naive child who could not possibly comprehend the inhumanity which is occurring all around him. All Bruno senses is that his carefree childhood playing and exploring with school chums in beautiful cosmopolitan Berlin has come to an abrupt end. He returns home one day to find his mother, the young maid Maria, and the rest of the servants frantically packing up the household -- clothing, toys, books, furnishings -- for immediate relocation to "Out-with," a camp in the countryside where Bruno's father has been appointed Commandant by "Fury." All his inquiries regarding where they are going and why are met with tense silence and grim faces. Only his 12- year-old sister Gretel, whom he calls "A Hopeless Case," responds by calling him "Stupid" for his mispronunciation of the name of the camp and his bewilderment as to what is going on. All he hears is that "Father" is an important man for whom Fury has a special job that needs doing. Fury has big things in mind for Father. Why then, does Bruno wonder, is his beloved grandmother so upset and angry with Father and why are his grandparents not moving with them? Once at Out-with, Bruno is lonely and isolated, missing his friends at school and his adventures with them. He is absolutely forbidden to explore beyond the confines of their house, but is intrigued by pajama- clad figures he sees beyond a tall wire fence which goes on forever. When he persists with his questions, Father angrily dismisses him to his room and Mother only says they must "put up with a bad situation." But he often hears arguments between his parents behind closed doors. One day, in bored desperation and hungry for companionship, Bruno ventures beyond his allowed boundaries. This one act of disobedience will put him in contact with a small Jewish boy Shamuel -- bruised, dirty, ragged, malnourished -- who lives on the other side of the fence. The same exact age, they immediately feel a kinship -- born on the same day in the same year.

This is one of the most gripping and heartbreaking stories I have ever read; and Bruno is indeed the sweetest, noblest child I have ever encountered in literature. Surrounded by evil, he remains uncorrupted, untainted by the monsters who operate around him and the society into which he has haplessly been relocated. Bruno, with his purest of hearts, will tug at your heartstrings. He is a most unforgettable character.

The Boy in the Striped Pajamas is intended for young adults, but it will have an immensely powerful impact on readers of all ages. Written in the simplest, most basic, unflowery style, its language and message soar and transcend ordinary bounds. Sometimes you encounter a book, such as this, so extraordinary in its honesty -- with a theme so real -- and a character so heroic -- that you can only sing its praises for its unadorned, but sublime eloquence. Utterly gripping, deeply moving, unexpectedly tender -- it is a masterpiece in highlighting one hallowed exception of man's inhumanity to man.

THE BOY AT THE TOP OF THE MOUNTAIN

by
John Boyne

A truly extraordinary story, *The Boy at the Top of the Mountain*, focuses on seven-year-old Pierrot Fischer, who after the deaths of his German father and French mother, must go to live in an orphanage before he is summoned by his young Aunt Beatrix, a housekeeper to an "important" man at his home in Bavaria. This sweet child yearns for both parents, his beloved dog D'Artagnan, as well as his dear friend Anshel Bronstein, a Jewish boy who resided in the Parisian apartment downstairs. At "Berghof," his new home in the mountains, he will be welcomed and nurtured by his loving aunt who gives him the name of Pieter, cautions him to act "less French and more German," and to discontinue exchanging letters with Anshel. These stern requests puzzle the boy and he is reluctant to comply. Little does he guess that the "The Master" of the house is no less than the German Fuhrer himself, Adolf Hitler, with whom he becomes fascinated. When "The Master" takes an interest in this fatherless boy, it is not surprising that he falls under the Fuhrer's spell. The isolation in which Pieter dwells, his lack of awareness of what is happening in the world outside this mountain retreat, as well as his desire for a father-figure, combine to make him easily impressed by the power he sees all around him. Gradually this innocent child will be transformed into an arrogant, rude, selfish, and bigoted teenager impressed with his presumed importance and dedicated to the cause of the "Fatherland" and the Third Reich. But not before, in his zealous embrace of Nazism, he betrays those who love him most.

The author is so skillful in allowing the reader to grasp, long before Pieter does, the destructive consequences of his choices. As in a true Shakespearean tragedy, we cringe in horror, knowing in advance the chilling events that are about to transpire; while Pieter unknowingly sets in motion an irrevocable sequence of events. The author arouses our sympathy for this innocent orphaned waif who is himself a victim, but also compels us to condemn his subsequent unforgivable actions. This book will have a powerful, visceral impact, much like Boyne's previous book *The Boy in the Striped Pajamas*. Both are unforgettable novels -- gripping, heartbreaking, and suspenseful -- writing at its best. The author's matter-of-fact, concise, and unemotional portrayal of the events is so incongruous to their horrendous and frightfully shocking nature, that the reader's distress is heightened to a taut pitch. Although ten years since the writing of the former novel, Boyne remains at the "top of his game" in this later one as well, a true master of historical fiction set in one of the ugliest periods in world history. I highly recommend this remarkable novel for ages 13 -- adult.

A PARIS AFFAIR

by
Tatiana de Rosnay

Very unlike DeRosnay's heartrending *Sarah's Key*, this more recent *A Paris Affair* is a collection of eleven short stories dealing with marriage and illicit romantic relationships. Each tale is prefaced by a quote of a well-known author or philosopher from the past: "There are good marriages, but there are no delicious ones;" "What greater pleasure than to cheat the cheater;" "If we are to make reality endurable, we must all nourish a fantasy or two." Each quote is chosen to fit the contents of the story. In one entitled "The UBS Key," a husband who has hidden his homosexuality from his wife for five years, confesses to her on a computer video and begs her forgiveness as he still loves her very much. Another is about a womanizing professor who seduces his female students. A third, "The Woods," focuses on a new dad who seeks his pleasure from prostitutes he seeks out in the woods as his wife focuses her time and energy on their newborn. "The Strand of Hair" describes the revenge taken by the wife of an adulterer husband after finding strands of black hair in their bed and elsewhere in their apartment. In "The Answering Machine" a wife accidentally learns of her husband's infidelity because their message machine recorded a conversation between the husband and his lover. Another story, "The Texts" employs the technique of the dramatic monologue which is similar to listening to one end of a telephone conversation in which the other speaker is never heard. Some are sad, some amusing, others ironic as "The Hotel Room" where the male lover slips a note under the door of the room in which his girlfriend is waiting for their rendezvous. In it he confesses that he must end their relationship; but when soon after he learns that the hotel is in flames, he is guilt-ridden assuming she is one of the reported dead. I don't want to spoil the "O. Henry-like" surprise that awaits him.

The book screams Paris with mention of well-known Parisian streets and landmarks. In addition, it emphasizes the French romantic stereotype of seeking multiple lovers and liaisons even for the married. Rather surprising is the way in which some of the jilted wives choose to handle their marital dilemmas. However interesting this book may be, it certainly is no equal in any manner to DeRosnay's brilliant and unforgettable masterpiece *Sarah's Key.* Perhaps it is unfair to even compare them, since this later book is an entirely different type of work, much lighter and far less serious.

LUNCHEON OF THE BOATING PARTY

by
Susan Vreeland

The setting of this book is the late 1800s in Monmartre (Paris) where the artist Pierre-Auguste Renoir is searching for the models, pigments, and location for what would become his famous masterpiece *Luncheon of the Boating Party*. This endeavor will be a challenge in many ways. First, he must secure a huge canvas, one with the largest width he can find -- two meters. Then he must negotiate the rental fee with the owner of the riverside restaurant where he wants to pose his subjects. In addition, he must get the assurance that those he chooses to pose for his masterpiece are free and willing to sit for the two months needed for completion of the work. These are monumental problems since he lacks the money to procure all that is necessary, including the expensive paints. Moreover, in order to become inspired, he feels he needs to "love" (to feel a kinship and attraction) to his female models which makes the selection process more individualized. Once work is begun, it turns out to be much more difficult than he anticipated. For one thing, the number of subjects who consistently show up keeps changing between twelve and thirteen, the latter an unlucky number for the Catholic jury members of the Salon where he hopes to display this work. Then one woman in particular, Circe, can't seem to remain still for long, turning her head this way and that, talking, talking, constantly talking. His patience is tried as it is next to impossible to capture on canvas all of these various people interacting with each other, eating, drinking, flirting. Artistically he decides to use one angle of the lunch tables, with the figures around it closely overlapping as several conversations ensue simultaneously. He employs foreshortening, the most difficult perspective to achieve. "How could he keep them all still? What had he been thinking? This number of people was unmanageable. Such glorious insanity! How could he keep them quiet, patient, cooperative, immobile when they had come to the river just for the opposite ... he needed to be an octopus to paint all these people and bottles and glasses, tablecloth, fruit, foliage, river, boats, opposite bank."

This book would be of interest to art aficionados as there is much discussion about the Realist versus the Impressionist schools, with mention of various well-known painters -- Cezanne, Pissarro, Monet, Manet, Degas, as well as Emile Zola's critiques of art. I found the descriptions of the various pigments lusciously delightful -- for one of the woman's dresses "ultramarine blue made from precious stone lapis lazuli, in the Renaissance used only for The Virgin; the mix of cobalt with rose madder for the gorgeous violet shadow in her skirt; and Renoir's careful attention to the folds of the skirt." Renoir attributed his sensory awareness of fabric, its textures and hues to being the child of a tailor and seamstress, at whose feet he learned the names of colors and was aroused by the sound of rustling taffeta. I loved the luscious hues -- it was a scrumptious delight: Veronese green for Jules' jacket, rose madder for Pierre's curly reddish beard, ultramarine for Cecile's torso, in addition to vermillion, magenta, yellow ochre. Also of interest to me was the description of the speed with which he painted -- "hand flew from canvas to tin of linseed oil, to his palette, back to canvas, back to oil, canvas, palette ... frequent turning of wrist to change the way of applying paint like a violinist changing the angle of his bow."

For those not interested in artists and their techniques, some of this may seem overlong; but for one who dabbles in art, as do I, and as a lover of words and imagery, I relished the keen description. While holding the palette of the aging, crippled Renoir, his lover says, "I wanted to touch his hands, the thumbs permanently bent against the palms, the frozen fingers twisted toward his wrist as weirdly as the olive tree branches, the knobs of knuckles stretching the skin ... thin as parchment ... I yearned to cradle them in my palms. I loved his hands, so small and brittle."

When asked "What do you hope people will see when they look at this painting?" he responded, "The goodness of life." In my humble opinion, when I look at this magnificent masterpiece, I would say he achieved that in spades.

THE RAILWAYMAN'S WIFE

By
Ashley Hay

Ashley Hay's *The Railwayman's Wife* is a story of love and loss set in Australia following WWII.

Anie Lachlan is happily wed to her husband Mac when, at the height of their joyous ten-year marriage, she finds herself a widow following a tragic accident on the railroad where Mac works. Here in the new location to which Mac brought her, she must fend for herself and her young daughter. The loss of Mac is devastating for both wife and daughter who try with all their might to keep his memory alive. As a means of financial support, Ani takes a job at the small library affiliated with the railroad company that employed her husband. In this capacity, she will encounter two troubled spirits, Dr. Frank Draper, who was one of the first to liberate the Nazi death camps; and Roy McKinnon, also a war veteran who earned some recognition through his poems about battle. All of these characters are struggling: Ani to survive without the love of her life; Dr. Draper to overcome his traumatic experiences; and Roy to find his voice as a poet once again. The setting itself -- the rugged, windy, sea town village -- is also treated as a character in its effect on all the characters involved. Ani has come to love the salt spray and windswept hills, just as did her husband. Roy has returned to this locale in order to recapture the wild, carefree spirit of his youth; and Dr. Draper has some unfinished business with Mac's single sister Iris. Moreover, he is crushed by the sense of his inadequacy and failure to save more of the Nazi prisoners. All the characters are broken or injured in some way, and each will have to find a purpose to go on. There is emotional conflict aplenty here -- and passion -- though not always clearly expressed and conveyed. All three are hesitant and vulnerable in allowing themselves to feel again. Read to learn how each of these damaged individuals copes with his/her sorrow and learns to go on.

VICTORIA

by
Daisy Goodwin

I love biography and good historical fiction, and *Victoria* by Daisy Goodwin is one of the best. Its subject is the longest reigning British monarch who was queen from 1837-1901, The Victorian Age, an era which reflected her principles and mores. Goodwin's excellent book begins with Victoria's ascension to the throne at age 18 upon the death of her uncle William IV. Until this time she has been protected and controlled by the wishes of her widowed mother, a German princess of the Saxe-Coberg royal family, and her mother's opportunistic advisor Sir John Conroy. Victoria has chafed under their restrictions and suffocating shelter as both consider her a young, naive, flighty girl in need of direction. Full of resentment for their close monitoring of her every action, she is determined as Queen to exercise her own authority and make her own decisions. Since she is totally unprepared for the responsibilities inherent in her regal position, she comes to rely on the handsome, debonair, and much-older Viscount Melbourne, her prime minister. They share a mutual respect and affection which soon turns to love, but marriage would be impossible given their different status and ages. Nevertheless, he remains her loyal and trusted advisor while others are working behind the scenes to find her a suitable husband. Eventually, one will be found -- a German cousin Albert -- who will become her devoted and loving prince consort. Much of the story revolves around the conflict arising from her love for Melbourne and the untenable position in which they find themselves. Melbourne has a keen sense of duty and is very aware of his responsibility to his country, but finds it difficult to reject this sweet and innocent girl whom he has come to cherish. There is intrigue aplenty here as various people of power maneuver a variety of acceptable suitors hoping for a political alliance between the Queen and one of their favorites. Even when Victoria does finally meet the young and handsome prince, she does not immediately take to him. Goodwin builds the tension and suspense as Victoria grapples with her decision regarding a husband.

I love the author's narrative style, particularly the dialogue through which much of the story is told. It sounds so authentic and adeptly conveys so many emotions -- hesitancy, discomfit, indecision, reluctance, regret, sorrow, to name only a few. This would be a worthy choice as a reading assignment for a British literature course since it makes history come vividly alive through the author's well-delineated characters. In addition is a deliciously romantic element that enhances the real story. What it totally ignores, which would provide good material for a sequel, are the tremendous changes that took place during Victoria's reign in industry, technology, literature, as well as the unprecedented population growth and its consequences. However, these later developments occurred after the initial period on which this novel focuses. In addition, I believe that Goodwin intended this to be a character study -- a portrayal of the evolution of an untutored teenager into a monarch and woman of substance -- and in that effort, she was extremely successful.

Victoria and Albert went on to have nine children. She afforded her Prince Consort great influence in making all political decisions, and she relied on his judgment just as she had on Melbourne's. Upon his death, she was said to be inconsolable, even laying his bed shirt out every night and sleeping with his picture beside her on his pillow.

It was said to be a true love story.

CALL THE MIDWIFE -- Volume 2
Shadows of the Workhouse

by
Jennifer Worth

Nonnatus House was a convent and working base for nursing and midwifery services for much of the first half of the 20th century. It was located among the squalid tenements that surrounded the docks in London which still exhibited the scars of WWII -- blown-up shops, roofless houses (still inhabited), and crumbling edifices. Living conditions were "Dickensian." Poverty, hunger, cold, disease, and illness were prevalent and spared no one. It was here in the 1950s that the author Jennifer Worth served as a nurse and midwife, keeping a journal of the work she did and the people she treated. She and the sisters ministered not only to the physical needs of their patients, but to their emotional and psychological ones as well. This journal became the basis for the popular PBS series "Call the Midwife," which was one of my favorites along with "Downtown Abbey" and "Selfridge." In the case of "Call the Midwife," as with the others, meticulous attention and research were paid to duplicate the real setting, costumes, characters, and situations. Actual events in history played a major role in each weekly plot. The TV role of "Chummy" perfectly captured the colleague by that name with whom the author worked: big-boned, practical and open, and with an ambition to become a missionary, which she did for a while. Sister Monica Jones, another main character, and her eccentricity and philosophical mental wanderings were so accurately portrayed in line with the author's description of the actual nun. In the book is a chapter devoted to the sister being charged with shop-lifting, much to the amazement and dismay of all her colleagues and townspeople. Since she is 90 and showing signs of senility, as well as having devoted her entire life to caring for this populace, most prefer to overlook these transgressions. Nevertheless, one vendor insists on a trial, one of the more amusing parts of this memoir. The witnesses called to testify all speak in a cockney dialect with its idiosyncratic use of grammar and idiom. As a result, the judge requests a translator to interpret what they are saying. For example, one cockney-speaking witness goes home to tell "me carvin' knife" (his wife also alluded to as "trouble and strife") about Sister Monica Jones pilfering his goods. The wife is incredulous to hear the highly respected and beloved nun accused and calls him "a Holy Friar" (meaning liar). Since she says she'll "knock him north and south" -- referring to his wife's skill as a pugilist -- he says "nuffink. I don't want my jackdrawer (meaning jaw) broke, does I?" which he feels she could easily do. The book is worth reading just to find out the outcome of Sr. Monica Jane's trial.

But little else is humorous here. At Nonnatus House the author meets Jane and the brother and sister, Frank and Peggy. Theirs is a heartbreaking story of being left orphans and raised in the Workhouse for paupers. Frank (age 6) and his sister (age 2) are inseparable until he grows old enough to be hired out to work, from which he becomes a successful fishmonger. His sorrow at having to leave Peggy is softened by the fact that Jane has also become her protector and friend. But Jane, an irrepressibly spirited 8-year-old whom the sadistic headmaster feels has to be broken, is the victim of constant physical abuse: flogging with a lash made of leather pellets positioned at the end of thongs to cut deeply into the flesh of her back, tearing the skin and exposing her delicate bones. She recovers from her unconsciousness, awakening in her own vomit, blood, and urine following this torture. Her only crime was calling a well-meaning, handsome philanthropist "Daddy" when he visited the orphanage, smiled, ruffled her hair, and called her "my child." She had once overheard that her father was a well-bred dignitary, a member of Parliament, who had had an affair with her unmarried mother whom he abandoned. So great was Jane's need for consolation, that she constantly fantasized about a loving father who would come and rescue her from this misery. The result of all this cruelty, in addition to having food withheld and being placed in solitary confinement in a tiny dark cell, changed the bubbly child into a mute-like creature. When the author met her as an adult, Jane was an anxious, fidgety shell of herself. As for Frank, one day observing a little brother and sister walking hand-in-hand along the wharves where he worked, he broke down in wailing sobs, for he had never forgotten his beloved sibling Peggy. Immediately he went to retrieve her from the workhouse and was heartbroken to see that she did not recognize him in the years that had passed. She was hesitant and fearful; but when he curled his little finger in the air, some deep unconscious impulse struck her as she remembered that they used to sleep closely side by side with their little fingers curled together. This is not the end of the story for Jane, Frank, and Peggy. Jane, for example, will undergo a miraculous transformation, from the sad and damaged child to a confident, capable spouse and missionary in Sierra Leone, Africa. That alone causes the reader's jubilance for her victory over all who tried to defeat the child's ebullient spirit. The author continues their tales, as well as those of others whom she encounters in her nursing capacity amid this very destitute section of London in the 1950s until its demolishment some years later. This is a book rich in emotion, replete with poverty and tragedy, hardship and unemployment; but what shines through it all is the indefatigable devotion and kindness of the Anglican sisters and nurses of Nonnatus House who do all in their power to better the lives in their care.

BEHIND CLOSED DOORS

by
B. A. Paris

Jack and Grace are the perfect British married couple. Jack, an attorney defending battered women, has never lost a case and is as handsome as his wife is beautiful and accomplished. Chic, stylish, a talented cook, Grace left a lucrative professional position to devote all her time to making her husband's life comfortable. He shows his gratitude by lavishing her with costly gifts, daily floral bouquets, and gentlemanly behavior, such as never failing to open the car door for her. His gallantry and generosity extend even to her sister Millie who has Down's Syndrome. It took little time to convince Grace to accept his marriage proposal when he suggested that 18-year-old Millie leave the residential school where she is a student to live with them full time in a magnificent dwelling Jack builds as a wedding gift for his new bride. Grace cannot believe her good fortune and is totally smitten as they prepare for a honeymoon in Thailand. It is in this exotic setting that she will shockingly realize the gross error in judgment she has made in accepting Jack at face value and allowing herself to be wooed and charmed by him; for her debonair and suave husband has a very dark side and is not at all what he pretended to be. *Behind Closed Doors* is a suspenseful, well-paced story involving deception, entrapment, imprisonment, and intrigue. Read to find out how Grace will have to summon all the courage and cunning she can muster to save both herself and her beloved sister.

ALL THE STARS IN THE HEAVENS

by
Adriana Trigiani

New York Times best-selling author Adriana Trigiani's latest novel, *All the Stars in the Heavens*, is largely based on the life of the glamorous Hollywood actress Loretta Young and the Italian girl Alda Ducci, who became her secretary and closest friend. The story begins when Alda, a pregnant teenager, seeks refuge at St. Elizabeth's Infant Hospital where, after having a stillborn son, becomes a postulant in training. After a number of years, the Mother Superior of this Catholic home for unwed mothers, decides that Alda is not well-suited to this work. Looking for employment, she is hired by Gladys Belzer as an assistant to her daughter Gretchen, better known as the movie star Loretta Young. This will be the beginning of an extremely close relationship between Alda and Loretta that will last a lifetime. Although Alda's primary responsibility is answering Miss Young's copious fan-mail, which increases as Loretta's star rises, her more significant role is as confidant and companion to Loretta on her many movie locations. It will be the frigid and snow-swept Mt. Baker in Washington state, the setting for the film *The Call of the Wild*, that will significantly alter the lives of both women. Here Loretta will fall deeply in love with her co-star, matinee idol, Clark Gable; and Alda will find a husband, Luca Chetta, who can forgive her past. Trigiani, the author, is adept at conveying both the intense passion and deep conflict of both couples. In the first case, Gable is a married man and Loretta a devout Catholic; in the second, Chetta is an old-fashioned Italian who is shocked to learn that the girl he loves is not a virgin. The book is peppered with the names of many former Hollywood greats who have a peripheral role in the story -- movie idol David Niven who becomes Loretta's staunchest supporter; Carole Lombard, one of Gable's five wives; Spencer Tracy, Loretta's first love; Myrna Loy, Rosalind Russell, Merle Oberon, etc. I am not a great fan of Trigiani, but I must say that this newest novel held my interest. Although her writing style is mediocre, in this one she has captured through her dialogue the clever repartee for which Young, Niven, and Gable were well-known. She also infuses them with a realness -- authenticity -- humanness. Despite their celebrity, she depicts these characters as quite ordinary people struggling with common problems: insecurity, fear of rejection and abandonment, concern about loss of jobs and income, desire to achieve, concern for family. Although labeled a novel, this is very much a true story of real people with great talent but also foibles and weaknesses like everyone else. If you are a fan of the silver screen in its early days, as am I, you are likely to enjoy this book.

IN THE PRESIDENT'S SECRET SERVICE

by
Ronald Kessler

There is a current problem in the Secret Service -- the high attrition rate of agents. It is not an easy job. Many complain of the long hours, stretching over days, weeks, and months away from their families, missing holidays, birthdays, and anniversaries. When they signed on, they accepted this as part and parcel of what some consider a heady, exciting, and coveted job. What most did not expect was the lack of appreciation and respect afforded them by some of the very individuals they would be risking their lives to protect. Read to find out which of the "First Families" were the most gracious and considerate, even sometimes delaying their holiday departures from the White House to allow the agents time with their own families; and which not only tried and tested the agents' patience, but also made the job unnecessarily difficult and even unknowingly sabotaged their own protection. One of these individuals demanded that the Secret Service agent carry the luggage and golf-clubs and threatened to fire him when the agent replied that it was not one of his duties -- he needed to keep his hands unencumbered. Which did the agents consider the "most clueless" because he summoned them to take his car to be repaired when it only needed gas. The same person called to say there was a problem with the garage door opener when in reality, the light bulb was out. And which child was able to thwart the agents' requests simply by calling her dad, the President, to get them to "back off." These Presidents are the most powerful men in the country, even the world; but in some cases they seem powerless to their children's demands. As Teddy Roosevelt once said of his feisty, outspoken daughter Alice, " I can run the country or Alice, but not both at the same time." You will find this true of some of the more modern Presidents as well.

THE HOLLYWOOD DAUGHTER

by
Kate Alcott

Kate Alcott's *The Hollywood Daughter* is a clever and imaginative blending of fact and fiction set during "The Golden Age" of movies. Teenage Jesse Molloy is infatuated with Swedish film star Ingrid Bergman whom she meets through her father who manages Ingrid's publicity at the David Selznick movie studio. She is so stricken by Bergman's ethereal beauty and is totally mesmerized by her screen performances in *Gaslight, Casablanca* with Humphrey Bogart, *Notorious* with Cary Grant, and *The Bells of St. Mary* with Bing Crosby. When this last film is set at Jesse's Catholic parochial girls' academy, she is especially delighted because it puts her in proximity to the actress. All the school shares the excitement, students and nuns alike since Ingrid seems the embodiment of wholesomeness and virtue, particularly after portraying French Saint Joan of Arc in the movie by that name. But it is a bad time in Hollywood since US Senator Joseph McCarthy, who leads the investigation on un-American activities, is accusing many members of the movie industry of being Communists. In addition, the Catholic League of Human Decency is banning movies considered sexually provocative or indecent. Both create intense stress for Jesse's father whose job it is to promote films, particularly, Ingrid Bergman's.

Compounding this pressure is the strain Jesse notices in her parents' marriage. While she adores her dad who is handsome, debonair, and fun, he often seems at odds with her beautiful, but strait-laced, reserved, and pious mother who is a strict adherent to her Catholic faith.

In this very good story, Alcott, the author, skillfully develops conflict on many fronts: first, the Catholic Church condemnations of the movie industry, which includes Jesse's dad; then between Jesse's budding maturity and all that the Church condemns sexually; moreover, McCarthy's witch hunt for Communists among those in the movie industry; the disagreements and tension between Jesse's parents; and finally, the exclusion from America of the brightest star, married Ingrid Bergman, for her illicit affair with Roberto Rossellini and birth of their "love-child." This scandal takes its toll on all of Jesse's family, especially her dad who eventually is fired with very dire results.

There are other elements, as well, that provoke suspense -- something secret and mysterious in Jesse's mother's past that seems to take its toll on her physically and psychologically. In addition are elements of glamour when Jesse is allowed to attend The Academy Awards. Most intense of all is Jesse's performance at a debate competition where she chooses to defend Ingrid Bergman, which has explosive consequences for all. Whether or not you are a film buff, this "coming-of-age" tale will hold your interest to the very end when, after shunning Hollywood for good following heartbreak, embarrassment, and overwhelming guilt, Jesse receives an anonymous invitation to The Academy Awards twenty years later. I highly recommend this book; which has a bit of everything: mystery, suspense, conflict, loss, romance, teenage angst, marital tension, movie star glamour, political intrigue, religious conflict, loss and renewal. You won't be disappointed

THE BOSTON GIRL

by
Anita Diamant

An historical novel, *The Boston Girl* is by Anita Diamant, the well-known author of *The Red Tent*. The main character, elderly Addie Baum, is asked by her granddaughter, "How did you become the woman you are today?" Addie's response to this question becomes the vehicle for the story of her life from her birth to immigrant Jewish parents in 1900 to the present. It was neither easy nor peaceful growing up in a crowded, dirty tenement in Boston's North End with a carping mother whom she could never please. She yearns to escape and experience life on a larger scale which happens to some degree when one summer she goes to a settlement house where she meets girls who will become life-long friends, as well as her support system in breaking free of her restrictive family. Although this was the "top pick" for book clubs by a library periodical which recommends the latest publications, it would not have been my choice. It is described as "absorbing," and although I might agree with that to a degree, I felt that Diamant's technique of the grandmother narrating her life experiences to her granddaughter resembled listening to one end of a long and drawn out phone conversation. The younger woman never responds -- there is no give and take. In addition, much of what Addie recalls is extremely mundane, like which sister used lard in her baking and which used butter. Moreover, the entire format of telling her story by answering her granddaughter's question seems contrived. I know Diamant is a popular author, which is why I chose this book for review, but "top pick for book clubs? I don't agree.

THE SISTERS OF HARDSCRABBLE BAY

by
Beverly Jensen

This book is appropriately named since it focuses on motherless sisters, Idella and Avis, living a "hardscrabble" existence with a depressed, demanding father and a silent, isolated brother.

It is a daily struggle to eke out a living in New Brunswick on a rugged, rocky potato farm supplemented by fishing for lobsters in the nearby bay. Enter a destitute Irish girl Maddie who appears one day begging for work which alters the family dynamics. At first the sisters resent her arrival; but since she shares their back-breaking work and has a pleasant disposition, they accept her. However, both father and son are attracted to her and find her a consoling presence with her sweet singing and delicious cooking. Things come to a head, however, where she and the girls are sent away to their aunt. When their father is badly injured, Idella and Avis must return to their poverty-stricken existence, but they now have experienced a better, more enriching life with which to compare this meagerness. "Part Two" begins with their move to the US, where Avis will tie up with some disreputable characters, while Idella meets handsome Eddie who becomes her husband. There are some comic, farcical scenes involving his eccentric mother, and the rest of the book takes us through their lives to the end. This is not so much a book to be enjoyed, as a tale of downtrodden characters who struggle with life's adversities, hardship, challenges, and disappointments in an attempt to make the best out of what they have been dealt. It provides a look at how little constitutes the lives of some with little resources and how mundane their existence.

WELL-KNOWN PEOPLE

SETTLE FOR MORE

by
Megyn Kelly

Gorgeous. Smart. Ambitious. Hardworking. All describe cable news anchor Megyn Kelly. In this autobiography *Settle for More*, Megyn traces her rise from a very ordinary and modest childhood to her own show on the FOX TV station. If she wasn't already a familiar face to many viewers, her position as moderator in the 2016 Presidential debates and the subsequent fallout with Donald Trump made her well-known. Megyn addresses the repercussions of asking Trump hard questions in that event -- particularly his previous derogatory and denigrating comments about women. As a result, she became his enemy # 1 and the victim of scurrilous tweets that went viral. She was harassed, insulted, and threatened by not only Trump himself but also many of his more passionate supporters. Her rise to the top has not been easy or direct. First, she toiled her way through law school, earning a prime position at a prestigious law firm and about to be named partner when she realized it was not at all that she wanted. The extremely long hours -- as many as 18 a day -- and the hostility and acrimony inherent in litigation were draining and exhausting to her body, mind, and spirit. Moreover, this lifestyle was extremely detrimental to her marriage and personal relationships of which there were few, given that all her time and energy were totally devoted to her work. When presented with the opportunity, she seized a part-time opening on a local news station despite the reality that she was sacrificing a very lucrative salary in this move. In addition, came the realization that she and her doctor husband had drifted apart during the years of their mutual devotion to their careers at the exclusion of all else. She describes the angst which accompanied these changes and reveals a very human side of her persona. In fact, she emphasizes her non-stellar teen years when the only thing at which she excelled was cheerleading. A key event in her youth was a prolonged episode of bullying by mean girls in her 7th grade class which caused her to encompass herself in a sort of shell of invulnerability. This would later prove to be an obstacle to getting close to colleagues and developing friendships. This is a very revealing look at a TV celebrity and the difficult road to success. She addresses how the sudden loss of her beloved father when he was 45 has affected her keen sense of mortality and propelled her to take action in the areas of her life that she felt were unsatisfactory. In addition, she finally responds honestly to the sexual harassment charges made against her boss and mentor Roger Ailes. In this autobiography, she comes across as an admirable woman juggling motherhood and career but always aware of what is most important; a devoted and loving mom who has her priorities straight; a principled professional who takes seriously her responsibility of delivering information to the public with a "fair and balanced" point of view which is the mantra of her employer Fox.

HANK
The Short Life and Long Country Road of Hank Williams

by
Mark Ribowsky

In this very thorough and well-researched biography of country-pop singer Hank Williams, Mark Ribowski captures the tortured and wild life of a man born to sing his heart out until it broke finally one day in 1953 at age 29. Born poor in Alabama to a dictatorial mother and weak and absent father, Hank grew up to become one of country music's greatest and most popular talents. Considered white trash, he sang like the hillbilly he considered himself to be. From childhood Hank struggled with daily pain from scoliosis and a degenerative back condition. Early in life, as young as 14, he attempted to dull his extreme physical discomfit in alcohol which he used as a type of anesthetizer. Not only was "Hiram" (his real name) self-conscious about his ragged clothes, absent father, and geek-like appearance (big "Dumbo" ears and thick eyeglasses), he was also dimly aware that the boarding house his mother Lillie ran, was in reality a "flop" house where men came and went to be serviced by the women who rented rooms there. Despite their poverty in these Depression years, his mother managed to buy him a Silverton guitar for $3.50, paying it off in fifty cent monthly installments, and to use a cliché, the rest is history. After playing his own songs in honky-tonk bars for years, this yodeling "cowboy," with the Southern twang in which he lamented personal heartbreak, infidelity, and constant struggle, managed to get himself to Nashville, Tennessee, the heart of country music, where legendary names made records and sang at the "Grand Ole Opry" -- Roy Acuff, Kitty Wells, Minnie Pearl, Jimmie Rodgers, etc. Hank's path there was not an easy one. Not only did he have to fight for recognition and a chance to audition, but he was in constant bitter conflict with his wife Audrey. Their hell-raising and physical violence occurred daily, whether at home or on tour, often resulting in injuries for both. She would egg him on so that in his drunken tirades he would shoot at her with a loaded gun. These battles became legendary in their love-hate relationship, but somehow it was mutually dysfunctional, both needing each other in some perverse way.

This book is replete with scads of information –- dates, releases of record albums, names of country music stars, their hits, the competition for placement on the charts and jukeboxes -- more than you could possibly want to know. However, its greatest strength is in its portrayal of a very talented "star," naturally gifted with the ability to write and sing songs that not only resonated and connected emotionally with his audience, but also conveyed with agonizing intensity the pain that was his everyday existence. It was amazing -- truly remarkable -- that given the amount of alcohol he consumed daily, along with medications and drugs, the rigors of traveling by car from state to state, and performing as many as four shows a day, he even made it to age 29. When he died of a heart attack on route to his next gig, he was emaciated, ghostly in appearance, gray in color, and unable to stand without being ushered onto the stage by two assistants and clinging to the microphone. The last years of his life were a series of cancelled shows due to inebriation, illness, stint after stint in rehab, and entire weeks of disorientation. His managers would simply lock him up to dry him out, then ply him with some miracle injection, push him onstage, and catch him when he collapsed. He existed in a drunken stupor for most of his final years, despite the fact that he married twice more, fathered two additional children, and continued to perform across the country though greatly debilitated.

This is the tragic story of an extremely gifted song-writer and singer, whose short life was plagued with physical, emotional, and dependency issues for all of it. In this book, the reader suffers with him, sympathizes with his addictions, roots for his rehabilitation, marvels at his stamina and endurance, and attempts to understand this essentially lonely complicated, troubled character. It's a fascinating read.

PORTRAITS OF COURAGE

by
George W. Bush

Portraits of Courage is an enlightening and remarkable collection of oil portraits painted by former Pres. George Walker Bush to honor sixty-six wounded combat veterans with whom he has become personally acquainted. The former President has declared that he intends to spend the remainder of his life devoted to helping this group in every way possible from raising funds to make their lives easier to petitioning for improved medical care. In addition, for recreational enjoyment and physical therapy, he arranges events, such as the annual W100K mountain-bike competition on his property in Crawford, Texas, as well as the Warrior Open Golf outings sponsored through the Bush Institute. What is quite surprising is that "W," as he is affectionately called, never handled a paint brush in his life nor ever demonstrated any affinity for art. However, following the completion of his Presidency, he was encouraged to try it since Winston Churchill, a statesman Bush very much admired, had found it an enjoyable and worthwhile exercise.

As a result, this book, as its sub-title declares, is "A Commander-in-Chief's Tribute to America's Warriors." Accompanying each portrait, is a narrative about that soldier's childhood, military experience, subsequent injuries, coping strategies, and present status. The suffering and multiple surgeries that many have had to endure are indicative of their courage, fortitude, and sheer tenacity.

Theirs are heart-rending experiences; but despite all, those who were able returned to active duty willingly, intent on getting back to their buddies in fighting terrorism and injustice. I found their strength, integrity, dedication and love of country truly inspiring. After rehabilitation, many just wanted to get back on their feet again to continue their lives with their families. Also heart-warming is the unconditional love and undying support provided by their wives and children who refuse to see their loved ones as victims, but rather as true American heroes, which indeed they are. Theirs is not an entirely rosy picture, however, since many, in addition to physical challenges and amputations, have also suffered traumatic head injuries, stress disorder, nightmares, migraines, depression, and memory loss. But by and large, each declares -- especially the Marines -- *Sempre Fidelis* – "always faithful" to God, country, and also their partner whom one Marine Corporal David Smith says is "his source of strength and inspiration. Everything about her makes me want to be a better man." So many have gone on to lead worthwhile, productive lives, as Staff Sergeant James Stanek, Jr.: "My mission since I left the service has been to help my brothers and sisters in need. I am out of the war, but I am not out of the fight. I will not quit." Another, Lt. Col. Kenneth Dwyer, now executive officer of the Special Warfare Training Group at Ft. Bragg, asserted, "I have the greatest job in the world. I get to go to work every day with guys who are willing to sacrifice their lives for me...I don't think you can find that anywhere else." These men have not allowed their problems to defeat them. One successfully manages a golf course in Mississippi; another works with the "Wounded Warriors" organization; one is a physician's assistant; so many continued their education -- a doctorate from Baylor University, a BA in business administration, an MBA, etc.

    In many cases these warriors were from military families in which multiple generations had dedicated their lives to their country. I know this sounds like a cliché, but this book so deeply impressed upon me the gratitude, and respect we owe those who sacrifice their own comfort and well-being for our protection. They have given the ultimate, and I applaud former Pres. Bush who states on the last page how very much he "cares about them ... and will until the day I die." His respect and affection for these courageous men jumps off the page as almost palpable.

A FRIEND OF MR. LINCOLN

by
Stephen Harrigan

A compelling novel steeped in history, *A Friend of Mr. Lincoln,* focuses on the relationship between the fictional character Cage Weatherby, a budding writer, and an ambitious frontiersman, Abe Lincoln. They first meet in 1832 on the Illinois prairie as part of a volunteer group sent out to retrieve the "dismembered and disemboweled" bodies of fighters killed by Indians in the Black Hawk War. In this first part, the author is brutally graphic in his description of the battle and its aftermath. Cage and Abe share a love of literature, particularly poetry, and a desire to leave their "mark" on the world. Early on, Cage observes that Lincoln has a presence that draws men to him, a sudden burst of interest wherever Lincoln appears. Lincoln is a unique character, a gangly backwoodsman who quotes the Romantic Age poet Lord Byron, as well as holding others in rapt attention with his ribald jokes and bawdy tales. Most of the story takes place in Springfield, Illinois, the stage of political power as it becomes the state capitol. Their friendship will be tested in numerous ways. First, Cage has abolitionist sentiments to which the young Abe is not yet committed. In addition, Cage is disturbed by Abe's penning anonymous newspaper articles, under the guise of "Sampson's Ghost," to assassinate the characters of his opponents. Cage considers it cowardly and ignoble, only one way in which the author portrays Lincoln as a less heroic figure than have other writers. Harrigan has taken liberties aplenty. For example, Lincoln's tendency toward melancholia has been revealed in well-researched biographies, but Harrigan has him suffer a full-blown nervous breakdown over his indecision to marry Mary Todd. Cage actually tries to dissuade Lincoln from this alliance, which he says "will ruin" Abe. Cage finds her a manipulative, conniving, flirtatious tease who will be "ever plotting, wanting, needing more" from her husband. As a result, Mary considers Cage an enemy, even at this early stage, and will eventually exact her revenge in a most malicious manner. Lincoln's association with this cunning woman is not the only time the author shows Lincoln full of despair -- drowning in a catatonic, morose malaise.

Along with Mary Todd is depicted another female character, the independent, feminist Emma who becomes Cage's lover, but refuses to become his wife, or anyone else's. Their romance, a sort of "cat and mouse game," provides another layer to the tale. In addition is an excellent courtroom trial scene with Lincoln the defender of a guilty man that so enrages Cage to the point of ending their friendship. Despite Cage's forewarnings of a tempestuous marriage, the equally ambitious Mary Todd has set her sights on "a man who is going places" where she wants to go too, and finally secures her desire to become his wife. This is a many tiered book, a look at the various stages in Lincoln's rise to the Presidency. Moreover, it is an intimate look at the man himself, especially his contradictions that so puzzle his best friend. The author begins the book with Lincoln's funeral, a sober and darkly-shrouded event, then flashes back to earlier times. Stephen Harrigan has succeeded in a skillfully wrought tale of two friends whose shared ambition is "to live a life of consequence." At the same time, he allows a totally absorbing peek into their private lives.

THE GOOD SON
JFK, Jr. and the Mother He Loved

by
Christopher Andersen

In case you are likely to dismiss this biography by *New York Times* Best-selling author, Christopher Andersen, as another "tell-all" gossip tale about the scandalous escapades of the legendary Kennedy family, consider that this book focuses refreshingly on one particular member who never demonstrated any egregiously bad behavior, rudeness, attitude, or social superiority -- namely JFK, Jr. In fact, relying on interviews with Secret Service agents, nannies, flight instructors, classmates, teachers, even most photographers and newspaper men -- those who knew him best or observed him closely-- the author portrays John as a self-effacing, likeable, personable, down-to-earth young man who handled his celebrity with grace and dignity. Despite a privileged life as the adored son of Jacqueline Bouvier Kennedy and President John Kennedy, all who knew him considered him unspoiled, devoid of egotism, and humble in his attempt and desire to be just a regular guy. Although there is repetition of much that we already know about his mother and her relationship with Aristotle Onassis, about his rambunctious cousins (children of RFK and Ethel Kennedy), about Uncle Ted, this is the first book I've read that tries to reveal the person behind the "persona," and John, Jr. comes off looking admiringly good in character, decency, and deportment. His one tragic flaw was a sort of ADD which caused difficulty with concentration for long periods of time. He was always in motion -- roller-skating, biking, flying, etc. He could be seen on any day on any New York street or in Central Park whizzing by like any other energetic athlete, trying his best to blend-in, never seeking the lime-light, always trying to maintain his privacy, a nearly impossible desire given who he was. Also admirable and touching was his very close relationship and bond with his mother, which the author conveys in poignant anecdotes. Once the reader feels he knows this handsome, charming rising "star" with limitless potential, John's sudden premature death with his new bride in an airplane he was piloting seems all the more tragic. You might not want to skip this one, since it reveals an individual of integrity and substance who was trying his best to forge his way in life, find his own path, and succeed on his own terms.

ROSEMARY
The Hidden Kennedy Daughter

by
Kate Clifford Larson

Heartbreaking, poignant, yet very revealing is Kate Larson's biography of Rosemary Kennedy, the third child and first daughter of the famous Joe and Rose Kennedy's family of nine children. At a time when mental-retardation carried a stigma, Rosemary's condition remained publicly unacknowledged during her childhood and adolescence in this group of high achievers that eventually included a US President, a number of US Senators, a Congressman, a prominent newswoman and TV celebrity, ambassadors to foreign countries, a magazine publisher, as well as powerful advocates for Special Olympics. Considered the most beautiful and attractive of all the Kennedys, she nonetheless demonstrated a much slower development, both intellectual and physical, compared to her highly competitive brothers and sisters. The author catalogues the many attempts of her parents to secure the best physicians and schools to accommodate her needs and develop her potential to the fullest. No expense was spared. Both mother and father continually researched the latest facilities, programs, theories -- both here and abroad -- in order to provide her with the best treatments available. However, as she reached adulthood, her limitations, outbursts, and frequent nocturnal wanderings became a cause of great concern for her safety, as well as the public image of this illustrious family. Disappointed in her lack of improvement despite years of special care, therapy, and instruction, her father Joe decided to follow the recommendation of two prominent doctors whose suggestion was a lobotomy presented as a possible "cure" for Rosemary's disabilities. Following the surgery, Rosemary deteriorated and became only a mute "shell" of her former self, although she lived to reach 86. This is a moving tale of a family's struggle, grief, loss, and, in this case, guilt regarding this decision for their daughter. All were traumatized by the result of the surgery, no one less than Rosemary herself. In the aftermath, denial and secrecy prevailed, especially as the political aspirations of her brothers rose, and Rosemary was sequestered in a number of revolving Catholic institutions where nuns were assigned to her daily care. A careful and meticulous researcher, Larson had the advantage of access to previously restricted correspondence between the young Rosemary and her parents, as well as numerous letters between the parents and Rosemary's doctors and caregivers. The sadness of Rosemary's fate is underscored by the sweet and loving missives from a lonely girl so eager for the approval and acceptance of her parents. These authentic letters from Rosemary reveal a very sensitive, endearing, lovable young girl frustrated by her limitations and at the mercy of her misguided parents. Larson does not assign blame for Rosemary's tragedy, but instead narrates the events that led up to it. Her contention seems to be that Rosemary -- rather than having the least impact -- may well be the one whose condition most influenced her brother Ted's work toward the passing of the Education for All Handicapped Children Act (1975) and the Americans with Disabilities Act (1990). In addition, two previous important pieces of legislation for the intellectually disabled were signed by her brother Pres. John Kennedy in 1961 just weeks before his death. Moreover, her sister Eunice Shriver's deep devotion to Rosemary also generated Eunice's life's work for Special Olympics.

A LUCKY LIFE INTERRUPTED

by
Tom Brokaw

A very personal and intimate "memoir of hope," *A Lucky Life Interrupted* is news-anchor and journalist Tom Brokaw's narration of his journey in dealing with a life-threatening illness, multiple myeloma. A treatable but incurable type of blood cancer, MM first manifested itself as a persistent, chronic backache of a year's duration. An active outdoorsman and frequent flyer, Brokaw (age 73) at first attributed the pain to too much rock-climbing, bike-riding, pheasant hunting, fishing thigh-deep in powerful waters and streams, as well as too many long plane trips. The first two highly-esteemed orthopedic specialists he consulted did not find anything seriously wrong, but his primary care/internist did blood tests which revealed MM. Fortunately, Tom's daughter is an emergency room physician who was able to interpret for him the inundation of information he was being presented regarding his diagnosis, options for treatment, and prognosis. This is an extremely frank description of the shock of learning one has cancer ("C'mon, this doesn't happen to me at 73") and the myriad emotions and confusion that accompany that unsettling news. For a long time, he chose to keep it private, sharing his illness with only his wife Meredith and immediate family. He cites their devotion and support as the main gift in getting through difficult treatments, extreme fatigue, melancholy, and immobilizing pain. The voice of the speaker is not the self-assured, confident newsman we were accustomed to seeing on TV's *NBC Nightly News*, but a much more vulnerable human being dealing with the indignity of being powerless and much changed in appearance. Most sobering is the realization that despite the best care from renowned physicians at Memorial Sloan Kettering (NY), Dana Farber Institute (Boston), and The Mayo Clinic (Rochester, Minnesota), the outcome is uncertain. Nevertheless, after the first startling consultation, he does not bemoan his fate with questions like

"Why me?" First he acknowledges that he has had more than his share of good luck, both personally and professionally. His has been a great life! Also, he has the advantage of the best care in the US, as well as the means to afford it. The latest pill, Revlimid, which is being used to treat his condition costs $132,000 a year at retail. This prohibitive cost acquaints him with the fact that many other victims of this disease are not able to afford such treatment which then leads to discussion of "The Affordable Care Act" and stories of families bankrupted as a result of illness. Simultaneously, he also discusses the toll that Alzheimer's takes since Tom and his family are responsible for the care of a troubled brother Bill who had moved to a facility for this.

Brokaw presents a lot of information regarding MM, but at the heart of this book is a revelation of the character behind the perfectly groomed, articulate, composed and competent image. He is not smug about his success, but humbled that a Mid-western boy from a working-class background as he could attain the pinnacle in broadcast-journalism, and he is eternally grateful for that. We also see a very loving father proud and devoted to his family, aware that they are his greatest achievement. Of course, he relishes remembering the highlights of his career: visiting with the Dalai Lama, breaking the news of the tearing down of the Berlin Wall, his documentary on D-Day filmed on Omaha Beach, etc. But he is comforted by the "five reasons to live long and drink deeply of their love" -- referring to his five precious grand-children, "the next generation."

This is a poignant and honest description of his struggles as he adjusts and adapts to a new way of life; but despite frustration, uncertainty, and a growing acceptance of mortality, chooses to face his dilemma with optimism, surrounded by the love of a beautiful, cherished family. I highly recommend it.

THE CIVIL WARS OF JULIA WARD HOWE

by
Elaine Showalter

Julia Ward Howe (1819-1910) is best known for her composition of the patriotic "Battle Hymn of the Republic," although she penned other, much more personal works, including a collection of poetry entitled *Passion Flowers* in 1854 which was published anonymously without her husband's knowledge. Married as a young wealthy belle to Dr. Samuel Gridley Howe, she found her life transformed from a beautiful, intellectual, talented poet known in New York social circles as "the Diva" to a deeply unhappy, disillusioned and constantly pregnant wife controlled and dominated by her husband who sometimes called her "Child." He believed a woman should live only for her husband and children. Dr. Howe was well-known and respected as the director of The Perkins Institute for the Blind and had developed a method of educating blind children, one of whom was a young girl totally devoted and in love with him her entire life. In essence "The Doctor" became his wife's jailer with his constant restrictions, particularly regarding her writing, adamantly opposing any outlet for her creativity. In this marriage, she began to feel confined, depressed, and hopeless which she confided to her sister in letters. Her husband even forbade the use of ether during the birth of her children (of which there were six). He asserted that women needed discipline, insisting that a female of sound and healthy constitution need not rely on such anesthetics. (Note: he was seldom there throughout her labors, sometimes arriving just in time to cut the umbilical cord.) She lamented in a missive to her sister Wevie: "Are we meant to change so utterly? ... Are our hearts to fade out with our early bloom, and, in giving life to others, do we lose our vitality, and sink into dimness, nothingness, and living death?" She had lost all confidence in herself and feared she would never write again. Not only did she suffer an insensitive, egotistical husband who felt his way was the only way, moving into homes which he knew she found dreary and isolating, but he even took control of her fortune which he squandered on bad investments. Even when she earned some meager income from her articles, she handed it over to him as well.

For the public and for their children, they pretended a normal marriage; but there was constant stress, discord, and bitterness. After her husband's death, Julia took up the causes of women's rights and suffrage. At Oak Glen, her summer home in Portsmouth, Rhode Island, she continued her writing, a book on famous women, as well as hosting writers (Oscar Wilde, Mark Twain, etc.) and scientists to discuss botany, marine biology, astronomy, natural history, and literature. Her fertile mind was finally free to explore all the many subjects that interested her and attend cultural events in Boston. Eventually her achievements as a voice for "women's rights and the disempowered everywhere" made her a cultural icon. She had fought a lifelong battle for her own independence – her own personal, domestic "civil war" – and finally prevailed.

This is a most enlightening book revealing the trials and tribulations of a remarkable, talented woman with a first-rate mind who was relegated to the sidelines by her husband and society, as well as forced into the strictly proscribed role of a woman at that time -- secondary, unacknowledged, subservient. In fact, the renowned writer Nathaniel Hawthorne declared that Howe should have been "soundly whipt for publishing *Passion Flowers"* because in it she dared to express her unhappiness with marriage. This is an exceptionally well-written, well-researched biography of this under-rated female activist and writer. The author's reliance on Howe's personal letters, as well as interviews with her children, provide keen insight into the conflicting feelings and struggles of this oppressed woman and females of her generation. Her ambivalence regarding pregnancy and motherhood have a universality that will certainly resonate with many present-day mothers. *The Civil Wars of Julia Ward Howe* very successfully depicts the evolution of a key figure of her era from subjugated wife to an independent and powerful reformer in her own right.

BOYS IN THE TREES: A MEMOIR

by
Carly Simon

    The focus of this book, *Boys in the Trees*, is singer and songwriter Carly Simon's lifelong battle with anxiety, depression, and low self-esteem. She is able to trace her vulnerability back to her early childhood when it first manifested itself in stuttering. After all remedies failed, her mother suggested that Carly attempt to sing the words she was struggling to pronounce, and, in a sense, that was the beginning of her musical career. The daughter of Richard Simon, the brilliant and innovative publisher who started the successful partnership of Simon & Shuster, Carly always felt "unworthy and unloved." Surrounded by two "bird-of-paradise" sisters, an attractive mother, and numerous high-powered and glamorous couples who were frequent guests at the family homes in Stamford, Connecticut; New York City; and the island of Martha's Vineyard, Carly always felt lacking in comparison to others -- "not pretty enough, not smart enough, not witty enough." For much of her young adulthood, she studied other girls to model -- how to speak, how to dress, how to dance." Nevertheless, she remained insecure -- "a bundle of nerves, a walking pile of needs and conflicts." Many of her recollections are taken verbatim from old diaries she kept through her youth which reveal a shy, scared, wounded girl with an overwhelming desire to be noticed, appreciated, and accepted unconditionally. Eventually, it would be music that brought her recognition, but this success was not immediate. First, she tried college -- Sarah Lawrence -- dropping out to perform duets with her sister in clubs in Provincetown, Greenwich Village, and later in England. The high point in her life, which she describes in painful detail, was her marriage to superstar musician James Taylor with whom she had two children. Theirs was a tempestuous relationship of ambivalent feelings, partly due to Taylor's drug and alcohol abuse, as well as sexual infidelity. Angry, resentful, and heartbroken, Carly retaliated with romantic affairs of her own. Eventually, her disappointment and disillusionment took its toll both physically and emotionally; she suffered a breakdown, and the union ended in divorce. In addition to the very personal confessions of the author, her book expresses her love for the island of Martha's Vineyard where she and Taylor built a home in which she still resides. Having spent time there since childhood, she feels a kinship with its landscape and also derives inspiration for her music. It is an integral part of her life, both her joys and her sorrows. *Boys in the Trees* is a painfully revealing book of personal introspection and analyses of dysfunctional relationships by a very talented, accomplished, and sensitive artist in the world of popular music.

SHIRLEY JACKSON
A Rather Haunted Life

by
Ruth Franklin

Eerie! Spooky! Uncanny! Shocking! Savage! Misanthropic! These adjectives describe the work of Shirley Jackson, a literary master of the short story. Shirley first attracted attention in 1942 with the publication of "The Lottery" which focuses on a brutal ancient rite practiced in an ordinary rural town. On a particular day each year, the inhabitants gather to participate in a traditional lottery in which the head of each household draws a number from a hat to indicate which family has been selected as the "winner." Then it is narrowed down, again by choosing a number, as to which member of that particular family is the "chosen" one. All of this takes place on a beautiful sunny day with families rushing to the local gathering place, everyone eager and excited, exchanging pleasantries and gossip. The gruesome surprise at the end is that the one drawing the unlucky number is be stoned to death by the community members, including children. The awful outcome is so incongruous to the happy and casual mood set at the beginning, that the reader is left horrified. This story catapulted Jackson to fame although it was received with some extremely negative criticism by the reading public who found it enigmatic and difficult to understand. More stories and novels were written in the same vein although Jackson was also capable of writing motherly, domestic tales about adorable children, such as "Charles" in which she uses her own small son Laurie as a character. As a writer, she seemed a dichotomy -- a dual persona -- an ordinary housewife and loving mother of four while simultaneously an author of intensely angry and violent tales, such as *The Haunting of Hill House*. Shirley was indeed an embittered woman having been raised by a critical, harping mother who constantly belittled her daughter's appearance and obesity, her sloppy habits and slovenly housekeeping, her unconventional dress. Additional pressure came from her husband

Stanley Hyman, a brilliant literary critic, who recognized her talent but also constantly pressured her to produce since she was the main breadwinner. He resented her success while admiring her genius, and caused her great emotional and psychic pain from his infidelities with students at Bennington College in Vermont where he was a professor. Shirley and her children became emotionally alienated and isolated from their small-town neighbors who considered them strange and outlandish. Of course, the unusual subject matter of Shirley's literature confirmed their opinions. For many years, her marriage to Stanley was a cycle of infidelity, fury, and forgiveness. In the early years, they seemed to have a "perfect symbiosis -- an intellectual partner who helped her realize her innate creative powers." But at the end she had come to loathe him and desire independence and freedom. The stories from this period are often about women wishing to run away -- to escape. Others involve matricide, probably a passive-aggressive attempt to excoriate her own mother. It is interesting to note that many of her main characters were motherless or victims of poor mothering.

This is a sad and tragic biography of an immensely creative mind who succumbed to substance abuse as a means to quell her inner anxieties and extreme desire for unconditional love and acceptance. Prior to her demise she drank heavily, gorged on food, suffered from headaches and body pain, dizziness, coughing spells, nightmares, fear of abandonment, and agoraphobia. Her main happiness was the "sheer act of writing" and her only comfort the "sound of her typewriter" as she let her imagination run wild on the page.

Whether or not you are a fan of her stories and novels, Shirley Jackson had a vivid imagination and was labeled "one of the first-rate talents of our time." This biography of Jackson's tempestuous life and internal conflicts is the best researched and thorough analysis of this unique author that I have encountered. One reason may be that not only did Franklin (the author) speak personally to all of Shirley's children and friends, but also had access to her diaries never before available. In Jackson's own words they trace her physical, emotional, and psychological deterioration. A powerful book!

WINTER

by
Christopher Nicholson

Many "Greats" in British Literature, although very talented writers, have not made the best husbands: Charles Dickens, H. G. Wells, Thomas Carlyle, to name just a few. *Winter* by C. Nicholson focuses on another to add to this list, namely, Thomas Hardy, author of *The Mayor of Casterbridge, The Return of the Native,* and *Tess of the d'Urbervilles.* Hardy was married twice, first for 38 years to a woman named Emma whom he seemed to love dearly; and after her death to a much younger Florence who felt he became indifferent to her, especially after making the acquaintance of a very young local girl, Gertie Bugler, who harbored aspirations of being a stage actress. Although 84 years of age when he met her, Hardy not only took a shine to the young girl, but became obsessed with her to the point of inviting her to his home and encouraging her to play the female leads in village dramatic productions of his works. He further encouraged her to play these roles on the London stage. His wife Florence greatly resented his affection for Gertie and objected vehemently to the attention he gave her. "NO! NO! NO! Impossible!" screams the hysterical Florence who serves as his secretary and handles all his correspondence. Angry and feeling taken advantage of, she finds it totally ironic when one of his fans writes to "praise his profound understanding of the female mind; even George Eliot (an equally admired female writer using a male pen name) does not come close." Florence is livid with this compliment of her husband and thinks, "Oh!... Sit down; let me tell you the truth."

Much of the book --maybe too much -- comprises a lamentation of her negative feelings: jealousy, resentment, rage, bitterness, hypochondriacal head aches and fatigue, melodramatic emotional breakdowns. She thinks, "I am a writer too," but her husband was disdainful of her childish poems about animals. She imagines that even the house they inhabit is hostile to her because he lived here with his first wife. She becomes hysterical about the heavy darkness created by the surrounding tree and carps endlessly about the need to cut them back. In addition, Florence believes that they were responsible for the growth recently removed from her neck, convinced that their spores somehow adversely affected her health. Constantly she feels "exhausted, body aching, nerves strung to a breaking point. I cannot breathe!" she wails. The trees take on a symbolic significance; she sometimes feels her "husband is a great tree and I am stunted from living in his shadow." In this way her desire to cut the trees back is understandable.

Each time she repeatedly brings up this subject, her husband replies, "Later." Her mind retorts: "I sometimes think 'Later' should be inscribed on his tomb stone."

As is evident, Hardy's second marriage was neither happy nor peaceful, and Florence Hardy was miserable. So many novels I have read about literary giants describe the same type of misalliances. So many brilliant writers, but so very unhappy! I find it ironic, for example, that Charles Dickens wrote, with such empathy, heartrending stories of the poor and abused as to bring his readers to tears. But his cruel and disrespectful treatment of the wife who adored him and bore him nine children, makes one wonder if genius somehow causes those blessed with it to feel they should not be constrained or regulated by normal standards of decency. Dickens even cast this faithful and totally loving wife out of their family home and discouraged their children to visit her. She forgave him everything!

In this book, however, Hardy's wife Florence, although portrayed as the long-suffering wife, does not come across as so blameless, benign, and ill-used a character as Catherine Dickens. If you can tolerate the plethora of harping, carping, self-pity and histrionics of Florence Hardy, *Winter* is a peek into the tragic marriage of a supposed "giant" in English literature, who although adept at writing about the lives of women, chose not to communicate with his needy spouse whom he basically chose to ignore.

MY WAY
An Autobiography

by
Paul Anka

If you were once a fan of Paul Anka, a well-known teen-idol in the '50s, whose hits included "Diana," "Put Your Head On My Shoulder," "You Are My Destiny," "Puppy Love," and "I'm Just A Lonely Boy," you might enjoy this book. It follows his career from his humble beginnings as an obscure, but talented kid, growing up in Ottawa (Canada), to living the high life as a performer in Las Vegas at Caesars Palace, the Golden Nugget, and The Sands Hotel where all the famous and beautiful congregated. There he played alongside the "Best": Frank Sinatra (who was "King" there), as well as Dean Martin and Sammy Davis, Jr. all of whom comprised the trio known as "The Rat Pack." Although much younger than they, he was accepted into their group and regularly "hung out" with them. From them he learned the techniques of music and stage presence, but also saw first-hand the toll of heavy drinking, cigarette smoking, gambling, and late night carousing. The book is filled with gossipy stories: of Frank's obsessive and eternal attraction to the sexy and torrid actress Ava Gardner; of his need to be surrounded by friends all the time; of his association with mobsters; of his retirement for which Paul wrote the swan song "My Way." Although much of this is well-known and Anka's writing style is mediocre at best, replete with clichés and repetition, there are interesting tidbits of up-close personal encounters with not only these "greats," but others as well: Chuck Berry, Elvis Presley, the Everly Brothers, Bobby Darin, Jerry Lee Lewis, Fats Domino, Buddy Holly, Annette Funicello, Dick Clark who created the hugely popular TV show "American Bandstand; comics Don Rickles and Joey Bishop, Michael Jackson, as well as Darryl Zanuck, the movie producer, and even an interesting accidental encounter with Elizabeth Taylor. The book is peppered with famous names, including Dodi Fayed, Princess Di's fiancé, to whom Paul loaned money; Teddy Kennedy and Al Pacino, both of whose behavior get an unflattering description; numerous well-known movie stars, business moguls, and mobsters. What is most remarkable about Paul Anka is the longevity of his career, the result of re-inventing himself when the times and music styles changed. His rock-n-roll music was displaced by the arrival of The Beatles when he was only 27, but he adapted to change in pop-music and began composing songs for others. He wrote the theme song for Johnny Carson's "The Tonight Show;" for the Welsh singer Tom Jones, he composed the wildly popular "She's a Lady," the lyrics of which he wrote entirely on a flight from London to NY, followed by the melody which he knocked off in an hour and a half when he arrived home. Despite his close association with people who lived "on the edge," over-indulging in every vice imaginable, he managed to stay clean and remain level-headed. The fact that he is still around, writing music, and performing with full vitality into his 70s indicates his musical talent, in addition to his ability to evolve and endure.

A PIECE OF THE WORLD

by
Christina Baker Kline

An exquisitely nuanced novel, *A Piece of the World*, like Kline's earlier book *Orphan Train,* is testament to the writing skills of this very talented author. In this one Kline focuses on Christina Olson, the subject of Andrew Wyeth's well-known painting "Christina's World" which geographically was a dilapidated old farmhouse in rural Cushing, Maine where spinster Christina lived a lonely, isolated existence with her unmarried brother Al. Stricken from childhood with an undiagnosed ailment, Christina's movements are awkward, her walk unsteady and lurching, often causing her to fall. As she matures, her condition deteriorates so that she is able to move only by dragging herself along the floor, using her hands, arms, and elbows to haul herself upward. As a result, she is bruised and scarred, but eschews a wheelchair believing it will only evoke pity, as she suffered when in school. In addition to her embarrassment, she harbors resentment against her father who denied this avid student and intelligent daughter further education in order to help her ailing mother run the household. However, in her brief time in school, she became acquainted with Emily Dickenson with whom she identified, feeling they shared "the chain" that severely limited their experiences. In the "vast emptiness" of the house inherited from generations of ancestors, she feels herself to be "forever waiting... marking the days by chores that need to be done the way farm families always have done." There are, however, two episodes that bring her to life. At age 20 when less debilitated by her ailment, she meets a young man to whom she is strongly attracted and who seems to reciprocate her feelings. Kline successfully conveys the hope, passion, and rapture of first love, and then the shock, humiliation and depression when Christina is rejected and abandoned after a four-year relationship. From this point on, she merely exists without happiness, light, or expectations. Until one day Andy Wyeth, an unusual man, the husband of her young friend Betsy, introduces himself as a neighbor living across the cove. Each day he rows over to paint the landscape from the Olson attic. Mostly he focuses on Christina's brother Al doing his chores in the fields, or paints the kitchen door with its peeling, faded paint. He seems fascinated with the house itself and soon with Christina. He senses a kinship with her in that they both "are not normal. We don't fit into conventional boxes." As they talk each day, her solitude seems less; and the wall she has erected around her heart begins to crumble. When he asks her to pose for him in the field outside with the house in the background, she accedes.

Of course, this becomes the famous painting we recognize as "Christina's World" in which mysteriously Wyeth captured her essence: "she floats in space… looking eternally young and old as the land itself: the sea creature sprouting limbs and inching up from the shore… her hair blows in the wind. Her face is hidden… leaning toward a shadowy silver house and barn balanced on the horizon line, beneath a pale ribbon of sky."

Kline is so effective in interweaving fact with what she imagines were the feelings and emotions of this uniquely challenged woman, Christina Olson. She adeptly gets beneath the surface of her subject's solitary character to provide us with an intriguing and moving portrait of a real person and the artist who recognized her uniqueness, successfully translated it onto the canvas, and in so doing immortalized her forever.

FICTION and HISTORICAL FICTION

THE GILDED YEARS

by
Karin Tanabe

It is 1887 at Vassar College where senior Anita Hemmings is rooming with wealthy and popular aristocratic Lottie Taylor, her best friend. Together with other female students, they enjoy their classes, field trips, parties, dances, and football games at Harvard, Yale, and other nearby universities. Anita has chosen Vassar over other prestigious women's colleges, Radcliffe and Wellesley, because she believes that in this setting she will gain the education and enrichment to become the sophisticated, educated, polished woman she aspires to become. But Anita is carrying a burdensome secret; she is partly Negro passing for white. This will cause many tense moments in this compelling novel as she attempts to hide her race in this elite world. Some involve her brother Frederick, a student at Massachusetts Institute of Technology, to whom Lottie takes a liking; others focus on Porter Hamilton, who pursues Anita and with whom she falls in love. Realizing his precarious racial predicament, Frederick fends off Lottie and warns Anita about the perilous path she is treading by becoming involved with privileged Porter who is unaware of Anita's background. Besides telling a story steeped in history (for Anita Hemmings was a real student at Vassar and the first black woman to graduate from that esteemed institution), this novel shines a light on an era following the Civil War when social and racial rules barred and limited Negroes from pursuing their ambitions for betterment. This excellent novel of historical fiction develops a number of themes: the miscegenation of bigots like Lottie who will betray Anita in the worst way; the comparison of racial intellect; the policy at that time banning Negroes from admittance to certain colleges; upward mobility between social classes; interracial marriage; the morality and ensuing guilt of betraying one's race by passing as something else. The author, a Vassar graduate herself, became intrigued with the history of this first African-

American female graduate of Vassar when she came across an old stack of alumnae magazines which revealed to her the history of a very fascinating woman, Anita Hemmings. In addition, the author is skillful at making these complex characters come alive as the real people they were with all their many conflicts. Also to her credit is the vibrant recreation of the opulent and elegant world of the upper-class at the turn of the century. It is a book worth reading.

LILLI de JONG

by
Janet Benton

A book of historical fiction, Lilli de Jong refers to a young Quaker woman who finds herself pregnant and unwed in 1883 Philadelphia. Believing herself abandoned by Johan, the father of her baby, and grieving the loss of her recently deceased mother, Lilli flees and seeks refuge in the Haven for Women and Infants. Throughout all her trials and tribulations, Lilli confides her deepest feelings and fears to her diary, which becomes the form of the book. It is expected that upon the birth of her baby, the new mother will relinquish her child for adoption; but in this case, Lilli is overcome with such love for her child that she is unable to separate from her tiny daughter Charlotte. For a time, she is employed by a wealthy family to nurse their newborn son while she must consign her own child to a wet nurse. Her time with the wealthy Burnhams is fraught with problems. Mrs. Burnham, feeling no affection for her frail and fretful son Henry, shuns her maternal duties leaving him entirely in Lilli's care. In addition, Lilli is given a major share of the household maintenance, overworked and underpaid. Then she must fend off Mr. Burnham's sexual advances. Frantic with worry for her own child, when she finds her daughter Charlotte wasting away in a slum shack neglected by an irresponsible caretaker, she rescues the child and flees with her. So begins Lilli's descent into poverty and homelessness, preyed upon by thieves and miscreants. Her misery and despair is exacerbated by the betrayal of Johan who seemed to truly love her, vowing to summon her after he had established himself in the city.

The author focuses almost entirely on Lilli's plight, first her shame and the disdain heaped upon her by all whom she encounters; then on her helplessness in finding suitable employment; her panic as she realizes she cannot provide for herself and her babe; her exhaustion and hopelessness when she is rebuffed again and again by those from whom she seeks support. Her story is not confined to the 1880s, but is the universal struggle of single mothers from time immemorial to the present day. It is the story of a mother's primal connection to her child, her determination to provide for it as best she can, and her refusal to be separated from it. The reader will sympathize with Lilli for all the hardship and pain she must endure and will admire her tenacity to prevail in keeping and raising her beloved infant.

GLORY OVER EVERYTHING

by
Kathleen Grissom

Glory Over Everything by K. Grissom, *New York Times* Best-selling author of *The Kitchen House*, provides us once again with a stirring story steeped in history -- that of Jamie Pyke, son of the cruel master of "Tall Oaks" plantation and his kitchen slave Belle. During childhood Jamie, who can easily pass for white, is raised by the mistress of the house, his grandmother, whom he believes is his mother. As her child, he is surrounded by luxury and educated. When he is thirteen, their mansion is destroyed by fire and his protectress dies. Since the cruel overseer is aware of his biracial origin and is intent on selling him at the auction block, Jamie flees for his life. So begins Jamie's acquaintance with Henry, a slave also on the run. This is the first of many harrowing and suspenseful scenes in this novel about one boy's journey to prominence and wealth. Along the way he will encounter many well-wrought characters: the elderly couple, Mr. and Mrs. Burton, who will not only give him refuge, but who will also provide him with an apprenticeship as a silversmith, and eventually adopt him as well. Another character who will have great impact on his life is the wealthy, well-bred Caroline Cardon, with whom he will fall deeply in love. Throughout all, Jamie maintains the secret shame and anxiety regarding his identity -- that is, until the already-married Caroline becomes pregnant with his child. This is a gripping story of heartbreak and tragedy at a time when bigotry and racism ran rampant in the South. There are other unforgettable characters portrayed in this novel, namely Suki, the speechless slave who can only communicate through signing because her tongue has been cut out. In addition are the widowed Mr. Spencer and his willful young daughters who will effect Jamie's escape through "The Underground Railroad" with such courage, compassion and strength as to turn what might have been disastrous into a triumph of the human spirit. The Negro dialect, in which part of the tale is told, contributes to the local color of the period and has a ring of authenticity. Moreover, rather than ignorant, illiterate, sub-humans, the Negroes who befriend Jamie demonstrate character, dignity, determination, pride, generosity, and selflessness. After a lifetime of running from and denying his true identity, Jamie will come to proudly embrace his heritage. This is a good book, well-plotted and excitingly paced.

THE SUBMISSION

by
Amy Waldman

The Submission focuses on designs submitted anonymously by architects for a memorial in tribute to the victims in the 9/11 bombing of the New York City World Trade Center. On the panel of jurists is wealthy widow Clair Burwell who lost her beloved husband in that attack. She is among those who favor one particular artist's version of a water garden for its tranquil and soothing elements that seem to make it a fitting theme for those bereaved seeking solace. However, once it is discovered that the winning design is the work of a Muslim, Mohammad Kahn, a furor and controversy erupts that snowballs into violence and hysteria. Concern centers on whether the families of the victims will be offended and that raising funds for its construction will be difficult given the name and religion of the architect. "Mo" is American born and educated, without any political or religious agenda whatsoever. Nevertheless, an opportunistic tabloid reporter, intent on "getting the scoop" first and making this "her big story," begins a series of articles distorting the facts and maligning "Mo." Her unfair and inaccurate characterization inflames an already tense situation and results in violence and attacks.

The governor too has seized this opportunity to promote herself in hopes of gaining votes in the next election. So many lives are adversely affected by the media frenzy -- one an illegal immigrant, Asma, a Bangladeshi woman who also lost her husband, a janitor, in the tragedy. She has been harboring resentment because the deaths of illegal aliens were not acknowledged nor listed at Ground Zero on the plaque bearing the names of the victims. She will face deportation when she speaks out about fairness and justice.

This novel inspires one to consider many issues -- moral, ethical, and political.

Should the panel change their selection given all the public hostility to their choice? Should the innocent but beleaguered Mohammad withdraw his design, given the animosity and opposition to it? And how do we address mass hysteria regarding Muslims? This is a thought-provoking book on many levels regarding bias, prejudice, fairness, democracy, individual rights, illegal immigration, improper and unfair media coverage, political opportunism, to name just a few. As well as providing an intriguing plot, this book will give you much to ponder.

COMMONWEALTH

by
Ann Patchett

Commonwealth, the latest novel by Ann Patchett, focuses on six step-siblings of a blended family. Their union starts when Bert Cousins, the father of four of them, kisses Beverly Keating, the mother of the other two. Following lawyer Bert's subsequent divorce from his wife Teresa and Beverly's divorce from Fix, her cop husband, the kids spend their time between California, where their mother lives, and Virginia, where Bert's parents own a farm with acres of land and woods which the kids have free access to roam and explore. It is on one summer day on this property where an event occurs that will impact the rest of their lives. The kids are "running wild" as is often the case when they are supposed to be under the supervision of Bert and Beverly. Son Cal has taken a gun found in the glove compartment of Bert's car, but it is not the gun that will cause the tragedy. Instead the Benadryl, which Cal carries at all times for allergies, will be misused with dire results. With the knowledge of his siblings, he gives it to their younger brother Albie whom they consider a pest of a tag-along. Often, this is their solution to getting him to sleep and out of their way. But on this occasion Cal is stung by a bee and has no more Benadryl to counteract the effects of the bee sting. All will suffer the effects of loss, guilt, and remorse for their participation that day on which their brother died.

This is a sort of "family album" -- albeit an unhappy family -- and was inspired by Patchett's own family. I have reviewed other books by this author, such as *State of Wonder,* which I considered excellent; but this one, proclaimed by some reviewers as "outstanding," did not meet my expectations. Other reviewers regarded it as "filled with wit and warmth ... richer and more resonant than previous novels." In my opinion, although the brothers and sisters survived the "aftershocks of divorce" and remained connected throughout their lives, I don't rate this her best work. However, I am in the minority since it has been on "Best-seller" lists for months and was called "One of the Best Books of 2016" by the *Knoxville News Sentinel.* I leave it to you, the reader, to decide.

MISS JANE

by
Brad Watson

A most unusual story about a most unusual woman, it is not an over-statement to say *Miss Jane* by Brad Watson is remarkable in many ways. It is the very sweet, exquisitely written story of an individual who refuses to allow a congenital physical affliction prevent her from savoring life in all its myriad aspects. Although born with a genital malformation, her heart, mind, and soul are miraculously intact and soar above the mundane limits of her rural environment. The story is based on the author's great-aunt who was born at the turn of the century on a farm in Mississippi to a poor family of laborers. Initially she does not attend school, but her desire for learning is so intense and her mind so sharp that she is drawn to further her learning, There she will encounter a young boy, Elijah Kay, to whom she will take a liking and who will later play a large part in her life. The most influential character, however, is an old country physician, Dr. Thompson, who not only delivered her and nurtured her through her first fragile weeks of life, but who also has remained deeply interested in her condition, as well as her general well-being. In fact, as she matures, it is only with him that she is able to talk frankly about her feelings, limitations, and fears for the future. On his part, he does all in his power to research the new developments in surgery at the big city hospitals where she might be "fixed." Through the years they develop a very close bond -- a mutually loving platonic friendship. Not that she does not experience romantic stirrings when in the company of the grown-up Elijah who is deeply in love with her. Dr. Thompson, in his acute perception, must intervene and explain with unflinching honesty Jane's physical impediments to marriage, leaving both heartbroken.

This is a deeply moving story, beautifully nuanced. In both Jane and her advocate Dr. Thompson, the author creates unforgettable characters, as well as an achingly tender portrait of an admirable protagonist who takes what life has given her and triumphs over her adversity, finding a noble place in her limited world. The pace of the story is simple and quiet, much like Jane's life itself and akin to the characters of Kent Haruf in his novels *Plain Song* and *Eventide*. Nevertheless, there is a serene dignity in Jane that transcends her humble roots and commands our attention.

THE WEDDING DRESS

by
Rachel Hauck

As is obvious from the title, this novel focuses on one very exquisitely hand-made wedding dress first designed in 1912 and worn by society bride Emily Canton in Birmingham, Alabama. There are two problems, however. Although the gown is exactly what Emily wants for this important day, it is the work of a black seamstress; and for that reason her parents deem it inappropriate -- a social faux pas -- for that era and their desire for upward mobility. After all, she will be marrying Philip Saltonstall, the son of a very prominent Southern family. In fact, Philip has forbidden her to wear the dress. Her more significant conflict, however, involves a former beau and best friend, Daniel Ludlow, who returns after an absence of six months. Daniel's sudden arrival stirs up uncertainty regarding her choice of a husband. He is dismayed that she has never answered the many ardent letters he sent her while training at a baseball camp, but she asserts that she never received them. I will leave it to the reader to learn how Emily handles her dilemma and also how the gown finds its way to a second bride, Mary Grace who is married in it in 1939 to her beau immediately before he is shipped off to combat. That is an entirely second plot which the author seamlessly works into the story by way of the gown. In total, the dress will be worn by four brides over the span of a century. The last girl, Charlotte Malone, will come across it accidentally in an old trunk she purchases at an auction. The lid of the trunk has been soldered to the base so that it is no easy task to get it open. Eager to know its contents, she instinctively calls upon her best friend Tim, despite the fact that they have recently broken up as a couple. Together they will be amazed and puzzled to find inside, this timeless pearl-encrusted satin wedding dress as fresh as the day it was made, as well as military dog tags enclosed in a small sachet pouch. Now will begin the mystery of the gown's history. This is a carefully woven tale of four brave and determined women separated by years, but all of whom have had their share of disappointment, tragedy, conflict, and doubt. Moreover, it is a romantic story about the difficulty of finding true love, but its abiding endurance once found.

MY NAME IS LUCY BARTON

by
Elizabeth Strout

Pulitzer Prize winner Elizabeth Strout has turned out another spectacular book with her latest *My Name Is Lucy Barton.* Achingly painful is the story of Lucy, a child raised in dire poverty by parents who are not only lacking in parenting skills, but also damage their children psychologically from a very tender age. The narrator is Lucy herself who is totally compelling in her description of her life, and the story begins in her hospital room where her mother has traveled a great distance to visit her very ill daughter. She does not come of her own accord, nor is she accompanied by Lucy's father; rather she is summoned by Lucy's husband who is very aware of his wife's intense need for her mother's presence, despite the fact that they haven't seen each other in years. As her mother rambles on about relatives, neighbors, and townspeople from their past, she is careful to avoid mentioning the very subjects which caused the most significant pain in Lucy's childhood. She never allows her daughter to confront her with the deep sorrow caused by her parents' neglectful and abusive behavior. She has a manipulative way of "tuning-out," closing her eyes as if asleep. This is a tale of harrowing human drama told from the victim's point of view; Lucy is astutely aware of her parents' personal limitations and blindness to the havoc they have wreaked on their children, as well as the ostracism and derision the kids suffered at school. Nevertheless, she can remember brief moments when her parents did show concern for their family, dysfunctional as it was. During the five- day hospital visit with her mother who refuses to acknowledge the most significant events of their shared past, the author is successful in placing the reader in the acutely painful and puzzling world of Lucy's childhood. Conscious as we are of Lucy's own internal state of being, we are nearly brought to tears for what she has had to bear. This is a deeply moving book -- the story told in simple and direct language

-- but the wrenching portrait of a girl's lifelong yearning for her mother's nurturing will leave you wanting to embrace her and make up for all that she has had to suffer.

ANYTHING IS POSSIBLE

by
Elizabeth Strout

I would describe *Anything Is Possible* is a sequel to Pulitzer Prize winner Elizabeth Strout's previous novel *My Name Is Lucy Barton*. In this earlier novel, the heroine Lucy Barton is recuperating in a hospital when her husband summons her mother because he senses his wife's need for maternal connection. But during this strained visit, Lucy's mother is unable to provide the tender loving care which her emotionally scarred daughter has yearned for all her life. Instead the mother talks around and avoids the issues which are uppermost in Lucy's mind. Suddenly, the mother disappears just as quickly as she reentered Lucy's life, leaving her daughter disappointed and frustrated.

This subsequent novel, *Anything Is Possible,* finds Lucy a successful novelist on a trip home to rural Illinois as part of a tour to promote her new book. It has been seventeen years since her departure, and her arrival will cause trepidation and inner turmoil for both her brother Pete and her sister Vicky. Neither has fared as well as Lucy economically; but all three have suffered from their impoverished background and dysfunctional family. Pete has withdrawn from society and lives an isolated existence in the dilapidated house once shared with their parents. Vicky is a bitter, troubled, and damaged woman who cannot forget that she was teased and ridiculed as "Icky Vicky" in school and that all three siblings were the victims of taunts and bullying for the weird outfits their mother sewed from scraps and the general disdain heaped upon the entire family from the townspeople. All three are still carrying the burdens of their ostracism long ago. At first it appears that Vicky harbors a jealousy and resentment of

Lucy's success; but when she sees her sister succumb to a severe panic attack just from being back in the family domain, she tries to calm Lucy and with Pete's assistance get her out of town and on the highway home.

There are many other well-wrought characters -- Vicky's daughter Lila who is a foul-mouthed, angry delinquent and Patty Nicely, her guidance counselor who tries to steer her onto the right track. Patty also has a sad past in this town. So many of the characters in this book are suffering from anxiety, abandonment, lack of self-esteem, and the remnants of poor parenting. They are in a constant struggle to lift themselves beyond the old hurts and humiliations that they have allowed to define them into adulthood. As in her other novels, Strout focuses on deeply personal family dramas, mutual hardships, and experiences that bind the characters to their past.

EVENTIDE

by
Kent Haruf

    Sublime simplicity devoid of anything superfluous -- such is the writing style of Kent Haruf, as well as the lives of his main characters, two older bachelor brothers, Harold and Raymond McPheron. Both are ranchers in rural Colorado, doing their work close to nature -- birthing and raising cattle and Black Angus bulls. Most of their time is spent between the barn and the corrals, except when they return to the house for food or sleep. They are reticent, independent men of few words, but of pure hearts and deep feelings. These attributes are seen in their sweet and loving interaction with Victoria Roubideaux and her baby daughter Katie. Victoria came to live with them when pregnant and alone, and they welcomed and provided for her. Now the young mother lives in the city where she is pursuing her education but returns on holidays and some weekends. The bond created between Victoria and the McPherons is strong and mutual -- they are a family and the baby is doted upon by these sweet men.

    If you are looking for swift action or exciting adventure, you will not find it here. The narrative is as slow as the brothers' drawl and their lives filled with mundane chores as they do their best to get through life and cope with adversities and disappointments, much like their neighbors. There is a quiet nobility to how they conduct themselves -- devoted to each other and Victoria and Katie, always willing to lend a hand to a neighbor. The unhurried pace of the novel matches the routine pace of their existence -- waking before dawn, working outdoors all day, resting only for meals and sleep. Night follows day, season follows season in a cyclical manner in sync with the days and months of their lives.

    But there is plenty happening in this story with a neighbor boy who tends to his elderly grandfather who SHOULD be taking care of HIM. Other characters in the story are the two young Wells sisters whose mother drinks daily and leaves the children to fend for themselves. Also needy are the Wallace kids, brother and sister of a disabled couple who can barely care for themselves, never mind their children. So many of the characters are suffering loneliness and in need of emotional connection.

In this novel Haruf focuses on plain-spoken, country people isolated by their locale -- who struggle to survive life's adversities and seek connection with others. The novel and its characters are noble in their simplicity.

THE DOLLHOUSE

by
Fiona Davis

"The Dollhouse" refers to the Barbizon Hotel for Women In New York City located in the neighborhood of Sixty-third Street just off Lexington Avenue. In the 1950s it served as the proper living quarters for young single females seeking training and employment in Manhattan as models, secretaries, actresses, writers, and other professionals. For a time it was the home of Grace Kelly, Joan Crawford, Liza Minelli, Candace Bergen, and others as they tried out their new independence away from home and the start of a career. Young men called it "the doll house" because pretty girls occupied its multi- storied levels. There was a strict class system: gorgeous models occupied the top floor; below them lived the guest editors for periodicals like *Mademoiselle;* and at the bottom those attending the Catherine Gibbs School for secretaries, many of whom intended to work temporarily while focusing on landing a husband. The two main characters in this novel are Darby McLaughlin, a Catherine Gibbs girl from Ohio, and Esme Castillo, a Puerto Rican maid there who befriends the lonely and naïve newcomer Darby. The chapters shift between this pair in the 1950s and journalist Rose, a present-day character in an affair with the married Griff with whom she is deeply in love and who has political aspirations. Griff will predictably leave her to return to his wife and daughters, which makes up a part of the story, leaving Rose rejected, heartbroken, and disillusioned. But the much more interesting portion deals with the elderly former inhabitants of the Barbizon where she and Griff have an apartment. One floor has been reserved for these older women who have chosen to remain there throughout their lives in rent-controlled apartments. In the lobby, Rose encounters the senior but intriguing Darby who wears a veil at all times in an attempt to cover the horrible facial scars from an incident years earlier when the Puerto Rican maid Esme fell to her death from the top floor veranda. Rose becomes obsessed with this mysterious accident and begins an investigation that will take many surprising twists and turns.

Although I would deem this light reading, it still has an element of drama and suspense which is maintained as Rose delves deeper and deeper into the relationship between Dabny and Esme. There are secrets here that are revealed gradually, exposed and unraveled through Rose's patient and persistent probing. Actually it is quite good for a first novel in creating suspense and holding the reader's interest.

THE DIARY

by
Eileen Goudge

A very sweet and curious story, *The Diary*, by "best-selling" author Eileen Goudge, begins with two adult sisters, Sarah and Emily, cleaning out their childhood home in preparation for their mother Elizabeth's imminent passing. In the attic, among other memorabilia, they find their mother's girlhood diary which, of course, intrigues them. As their mother lies incoherent in a nursing home, they turn to the old diary to learn more about her youth. Both are shocked and somewhat appalled to learn that their father Bob was not their mother's first love. Rather, the book is replete with Elizabeth's passionate attraction to a young man named AJ, whom Elizabeth's status-conscious mother considers "trash," an orphan being raised by poor grandparents, without any prospects of advancement. The mother is nearly apoplectic each time Elizabeth communicates with AJ whom she has known since childhood. Moreover, AJ is considered somewhat of a delinquent, having been involved in setting his uncle's car on fire, for which he spent time in a detention facility. But what puzzles them even more is that by their own observations over a lifetime, their mother Elizabeth and their father Bob always demonstrated a deep and abiding love for each other that lasted a lifetime until their father's death. For the first time in their lives, they begin to question how well they actually knew their parents. This is an enthralling story as the sisters delve deeper into their mother's past, picking up clues here and there, wondering how she could possibly have sacrificed her happiness giving up the one person she confessed to love so deeply and forever. By the end of the book, the women have a much better understanding of the difficult choices their mother had to make. A wonderful surprise awaits both them and the reader!

THE RUNAWAY WIFE

by
Rowan Coleman

An emotionally captivating story, *The Runaway Wife* focuses on Rose Pritchard who marries her husband Richard at eighteen following abandonment by her alcoholic father and the eventual death of her mother. Bereft and vulnerable, it is easy for her to fall for the mature and respectable Dr. Pritchard, ten years older, who offers her love and security. However, in the bargain he also has a pathological need to control her in every way -- how she dresses, where she goes, whom she befriends. Little by little, he creates an extremely restricted environment. But when his rages become violent, she flees with her little daughter Maddie to Millthwaite, a tiny village in the English Lake District where she hopes to reunite with a chance acquaintance, Frasier McCleod whom she hasn't seen in seven years. In his single visit home, Frasier, an art dealer, had been trying to obtain information about the whereabouts of Rose's father John, a talented artist. Although unable to provide anything regarding her long-lost father, she had felt an instant attraction which seemed mutual. She was newly pregnant, about which her husband was enraged, and struggling with doubts about her precarious marriage. Sensing her fear and discomfit, Frasier had sent her a note on a postcard of Millthwaite after his departure, but did not pursue her further as she was married and about to become a mother. When her marital situation becomes dangerous, she flees in desperation to that small isolated town. Not only does she become reunited with Frasier there, but also with the father for whom she has been yearning since his abandonment. This is a moving story of parental failings and regrets, the need to forgive and begin anew, spousal abuse and the need for courage to escape. One of the most intriguing characters is Maddie, Rose's 7-year-old daughter, extremely precocious and observant, whose deep understanding of their tense situation energizes her usually docile and passive mother to take action to reclaim their lives. In addition to the compelling main characters are a host of secondary but memorable ones who shelter and encourage Rose to reconstruct a new life. Their compassion and assistance are essential to Rose's recovery. Interwoven in an intricate plot are moments of drama, romance, discovery, and reconciliation. In Millthwaite, Rose will find peace in the beauty of the landscape, acceptance and support by local inhabitants, and a restoration of hope and love.

PRETENDING TO DANCE

by
Diane Chamberlain

A most interesting book that captivates the reader's attention from beginning to end, *Pretending to Dance* focuses on family, although the Arnette clan is a rather unusual combination of members. From early childhood, Molly Arnette has been aware that she is precious to all her family which includes her adoring dad Graham and two loving mothers, her biological mother Amalia, and her adoptive mother Nora. What is unusual is that they all live on the same family property in North Carolina along with an uncle, aunt, their families, and grandmother, all of whom have their own separate dwellings. Molly's dad Graham is a practicing and published psychologist who is in the final stages of MS for which he needs a full-time attendant/caretaker Russel, who is black but considered a valued member of the family. Just given the number of Arnettes living in close proximity to each other makes for an explosive blending of family dynamics. Molly has always sensed that some of her relatives do not approve of Amalia whose dwelling is a former slaves' quarters that resembles nothing like its origin. It is airy, fresh, and sparse and it is here that Molly takes dance lessons from her mother, a former dance instructor at a sanitorium where she originally met Molly's father who was practicing psychiatric counseling there. This is only one of multi-tiered plots and myriad subplots masterfully connected by this skilled author. First, is the complex relationship of Molly's dad to her two mothers. Then is the conflict between her dad and his alcoholic brother who is intent on breaking up the family estate for financial development. Next, is the ambivalent relationship between Molly and her older cousin Dani, a tough, unconventional, and independent girl who appears far ahead of Molly in maturity and who seems to hold her in disdain for her cluelessness regarding life. In addition, there are unknowns regarding Russel's personal life that Molly will learn about in bits and pieces. In fact, there is much that 14-year-old Molly does not know and her unawareness and naivete will make her extremely vulnerable, especially when she befriends Stacy, a worldly, loose teenager who will lead her into unchartered territory. Molly's family has a complicated history so she is struggling with their secrets, as well as her own budding sexuality, and a terror that she makes every effort to deny regarding the rapid deterioration of her beloved father occurring right before her eyes. Theirs is an extremely close and sweet bond, evident on every page of the book which makes their interaction all the more poignant. The reader senses the impending catastrophe that will turn Molly's life upside down and trigger an emotional upheaval that will cause her to flee for many years to escape her pain and sense of loss and betrayal.

Which brings us to the adult chapter of Molly's life after she has married a wonderful husband Aiden and they are awaiting the adoption of their first child. This situation will bring to the forefront much of the conflict from her past which Molly has tried to escape for years. It will also necessitate her telling her husband all about the family which she has tried unsuccessfully to forget. This is a thought-provoking story since it deals with parenting issues, biological and adoptive mothers, open and closed adoptions, innocence lost, unexposed secrets, unresolved emotional conflict, issues of trust, etc. There is so very much to this story that I recommend it highly. It will not disappoint but will surprise you over and over as it simultaneously tugs at your heartstrings.

WE NEVER ASKED FOR WINGS

by
Vanessa Diffenbaugh

This second novel by Vanessa Diffenbaugh, *We Never Asked for Wings,* is a touching and poignant story, most appropriate at this time since much of it deals with those impacted by the new immigration policies. Like her first book, *The Language of Flowers* which I highly recommend, this one focuses on a young couple in love making choices that will impact the rest of their lives. In addition, its characters are challenged by poverty, shattered dreams, disappointments, and a hostile society.

Letty Espinoza is faced for the first time with independently raising her two children, Alex (15) and Luna (6) since her father has returned to Mexico and her mother has left to try to find him. In the last sixteen years, her parents have dedicated their lives to Letty's children while she has worked three jobs earning their living. As a result, without their usual loving caretakers, the kids are frantic as is Letty since she has never been a responsible parent. But she LOVES her kids; and when put to the test, she will try her best to move them to a better location so that Alex, who is extremely bright, will have a better chance at success. But there is such a complicated history here. Alex is also the child of Les whom Letty never told she was pregnant when he went off the college and medical school. She did not want to risk ruining his future and trapping him in a marriage he might regret. Moreover, Alex has fallen in love with a Mexican teenager Yesenia, who along with her mother is an undocumented immigrant. His attempts to help her will backfire with repercussions dangerous to all of them.

The book is rife with the problems inherent in poor neighborhoods, with poor schools, dilapidated housing, stressed-out and over-burdened parents, lack of money and opportunity. Diffenbaugh has created a cast of very believable characters who will arouse your empathy and affect you emotionally, probably because there are so many in our country who are in the same plight and can't seem to get ahead no matter how hard they try. These feel like very real people; just as it appears they have some chance for improvement, their hopes are dashed again and again. But it takes resilience and perseverance and a sense of family to overcome the obstacles they face. Read to find out how two very decent men who should be rivals, combine their efforts to save these two families. It is an uplifting story that will make you smile at the end. It will also, in a sort of palpable way, heighten your awareness of the perils and terrors of being undocumented in this country. This is a story about love and sacrifice, forgiveness for past mistakes, and hope in an uncertain future

THE CHILDREN'S CRUSADE

by
Ann Packer

The term "the children's crusade" refers to the four Blair children's attempt to devise strategies that will prompt their disengaged and distant mother Penny to interact with them. Set in Northern California, this novel focuses on a family parented mainly by the father Bill, since his wife Penny has abandoned them emotionally and even physically by moving out of their home into a make-shift studio behind it to pursue her desire to hone her skills as an artist. Eventually Penny will move to another state altogether to achieve her goal. In part this is the psychological study of a woman overwhelmed by the demands of motherhood and feeling inadequate in comparison to her husband, a pediatrician, who seems to intuitively connect with each of his kids, providing them with love, guidance, and understanding despite their very different needs and personalities. The story alternates between their childhood and adulthood after their father has died and the youngest, James, a sort of black sheep, suddenly returns to the family homestead after many years absence. Always the problem child, once James returns his appearance seems to cause turmoil among his siblings: Rebecca, a psychiatrist; Robert, a doctor; and Ryan, a teacher. Gradually as they recollect the past, the reader becomes aware of their former dysfunctional home life and their unmet needs. For one, James has always felt like the outsider, probably because he sensed that he was the unplanned, unwanted child with whom his mother couldn't cope and for whom his father over-compensated. Ryan too, once a sensitive child craving closeness, seems even in adulthood, to seek this. The two eldest, Rebecca and Robert might have chosen medicine as careers in an attempt to emulate their steady and reliable dad and to understand their unreliable and deficient mother. But Packer, the author, seems to hint at one question: as perfect as Bill was in understanding his children, how well did he sense his wife's needs and limitations? Not only does Packer unobtrusively cause the reader to consider this, she also does a worthy job of making these characters believable and authentic, delving into their wounded psyches, allowing us to understand their behavior. It is only when they must come together to sell the family homestead that long held grudges, disappointments, and long suppressed emotions are released. If you like stories about complicated families, you will find this one interesting since it reveals how childhood experiences and relationships play a great part in determining our reactions to others in our future.

BASTARD OUT OF CAROLINA

by
Dorothy Allison

This is not a recent book, but certain works are so powerful, so compelling, so true as to be worthy of attention at any time and this is the case with *Bastard Out of Carolina*. The story is told entirely in first person, our narrator nicknamed "Bone," born in rural Carolina to a 14-year-old teen and raised among the close-knit, but hard-scrabbling, hard-drinking Boatwright family of extended relatives, considered "Southern white trash." Her uncles are well-known to law enforcement for their hell-raising antics and her aunts are nurturing mothers and wives dutifully tolerating, enabling, and cleaning up the messes their men make of their lives. It is with them, however, that Bone seeks refuge when her own home situation becomes intolerable. The innocent, silent victim of her step-father's repeated verbal, physical, and sexual abuse, Bone is in a constant state of terror, anxiety, rage, and self-loathing. She so loves and needs her mother's affection and realizes how precarious is their home situation, that she dares not share her secret agony with anyone. As she opens the reader's eyes to her bleak world and her sense of shame, hopelessness, despair, and disappointment with her mother's inability to shield and protect her, our fury toward the mother overwhelms us and our heart aches for this helpless child. In addition to the main characters, the minor ones are also carefully defined and depicted -- some eccentric, some pitiful, some despicable, so horribly flawed as to be worthy of our ultimate contempt. The book is replete with conflict -- emotional, physical, and psychological -- starting with Bone's utter lack of self-esteem and inner turmoil, her ambivalent feelings toward her beloved but weak mother, her abhorrence of her violent step-father, the shame of her disreputable family, her lack of normalcy or any way out of this hellish existence. This is so much searing pain for such a sensitive, intelligent, innocent girl, used as a scapegoat for her abuser's anger and her mother's spinelessness.

    The author's greatest talent is to allow Bone to tell her own story in her own language with amazing clarity. Sad though it is, this is a tale of resilience and survival; for in the end, Bone's feistiness prevails and she reaches a better understanding of how people are the creators of their own lives through their choices and actions.

THE SILVER STAR

by
Jeannette Walls

Jeannette Wall's most recent novel, *The Silver Star*, is a sweet story of the loving connection between two sisters, Liz (age 14) and Bean (age 11), but pales by comparison to her outstanding memoir *The Glass Castle*. Once again Walls uses a formula which has worked well for her in the past, the experiences of children left to fend for themselves by irresponsible parents burdened with too many of their own problems. In this case it is their single mother Charlotte who feels it necessary to take a "break" from them, as well as follow an opportunity to develop her musical "career." Hers is a world of pipe-dreams and unrealistic hopes of which her young daughters are very aware. Each time Charlotte's disappointments and inadequacies overwhelm her, she takes off, leaving the girls for weeks with little support, financial or otherwise. When she does not return this time, they manage to eke together enough money for a long bus trip to find their Uncle Tinsley from whom their mother has been long estranged. They have no idea as to what awaits them at the family farm which he inherited from his parents and from which their mother fled when a young woman. The reader admires the girls' resourcefulness and resilience, but there is not here the deep character development in Walls' *The Glass Castle*, but then again in that memoir the author was working with real and complex characters from her own life. Nor is there a substantial development of plot; the book reads more like a skeletal outline of how Liz and Bean take the initiative to decide their own futures. Although this is a poignant tale, the author seems to be cataloguing a series of difficult challenges in their lives and relating how they cope with some very sad experiences. I am a great fan of Walls and eagerly chose this book -- "novella" might be the more appropriate term -- because I so enjoyed her previous works, including *Half Broke*

Horses, but *The Silver Star* lacks the depth and quality I have come to associate with Walls. Still if you like a quick read about the tough reality some kids face growing up in dysfunctional homes, this might be for you.

THE HUSBAND'S SECRET

by
Liane Moriarty

This is a book about family secrets and their potent ability to disrupt and destroy the lives of not only the secret-keepers themselves, but everyone closest to them as well. Set in Australia, this novel has a very intricate plot involving a cast of overlapping characters and sub-plots. First are the Fitzpatricks, Cecilia and John-Paul, a happily married couple, and their three beautiful little girls. Theirs seems to be a model family -- Cecelia a super-mom and wife and her handsome husband John-Paul, perfect parents who are both equally dedicated to raising their children. One day while John-Paul is away, Cecilia stumbles upon a letter addressed to "My wife Cecilia, To be opened only in the event of my death." She recognizes the handwriting to be her husband's, and she is surprised, then curious, then overwhelmingly intent on knowing its contents. She speculates about possible infidelity, a second hidden family, homosexuality (since their love-life has cooled), or some former youthful indiscretion (since the letter appears to have been written long ago). She restrains herself for a while. Little does she realize, that once the contents are revealed, it will forever change not only their lives, but a great many others as well.

Not far away resides another happily-married couple, Tess and Will, and their young son Liam. Together this pair runs a successful business with the help of Tess's close cousin Felicity, who is actually an integral part of this family -- more like a family of four, rather than three. This unusual combination will lead Tess to doubt how well she really knows the two closest adults in her life.

Nearby lives a sixty-ish widow, Rachel Crawley, who is in perpetual anguish resulting from the murder of her 16-year-old daughter more than twenty years ago. Although the case remains unsolved, Rachel is convinced that she knows the identity of her daughter's assailant, despite the fact that there was never any hard evidence against this individual -- only that he was the last person to see the girl before her death. Rachel, like Cecelia, will also accidentally discover something that she believes is significant in proving the attacker's guilt. What Rachel does with this "evidence" will also affect many lives.

    The author develops a very intricate plot with overlapping segments involving these seemingly unrelated individuals. All will be brought together as the story unravels, revealing raw emotions, anger, betrayal, revenge, retribution, reconciliation, forgiveness, soul-searching resulting in new understanding. One of the characters says, "Getting married is easy; staying married is the difficult part." This story focuses on those in this story who find that statement to be only too true.

THE SECRET KEEPER

by
Kate Morton

A masterful storyteller, Kate Morton has skillfully combined war, mystery, romance, intrigue, and revenge in this her most recent and gripping novel of historical fiction, *The Secret Keeper*. In the first chapter the teenager Laurel Nicolson is lazily daydreaming in her tree house while the rest of her family is enjoying a birthday picnic down by the lake nearby. When her mother Dorothy returns to the house to get the "birthday" knife with which to cut the cake, Laurel witnesses an altercation between her mother and a threatening, intimidating stranger who accosts her. Many years later all Laurel can recall is the silver flash of the knife in the glittering sun as her mother lunged toward this man who recognized her and called her by name. The story shifts back and forth between the past and the present, fifty years later, when her widowed, 90-year-old mother is in the hospital living her final days. Laurel is intent on unraveling the secrets about her mother's past, as well as the identity of the man who was her victim. The chapters alternate between the 1940s, the war years in London when Dorothy was a spirited, daring, passionate young woman, and the 1960s, following her happy marriage to Stephen Nicolson. In her young adulthood, she had fallen in love with a war photographer, Jimmy Metcalf, and had "befriended" a wealthy girl Vivien Jenkins, married to a very controlling and abusive husband. But it will take Laurel many months and much investigation to understand those former relationships and her mother's rambling and incoherent pleas for forgiveness during her last days. This is a story with many twists and turns which are cleverly executed to deliver a mesmerizing story -- a romantic thriller with a puzzle to be solved regarding Dorothy's former life. Morton's depiction of characters -- Dorothy, Vivien, and Jimmy -- is superb as she drops clue by clue regarding their charged interaction in the war years. Much of the tale is clouded with suspense and tinged with tragedy as it wends its way to a most unexpected and shocking conclusion. This is one book that will captivate your attention throughout -- a real page-turner -- that will not disappoint.

SAVE ME

by
Lisa Scottoline

One of the most recent of Scottoline's seventeen novels, *Save Me* is similar to her other books in that it focuses on a legal defense regarding a suspected crime. However, Rose McKenna is not your typical defendant. Wife of Leo and mother of infant John and young daughter Mellie, she is a regular volunteer at Mellie's elementary school. One day while she is on duty in the cafeteria, an explosion occurs at the end of lunch period erupting in flames throughout the kitchen area. While most of the children are already outdoors for play, Rose has kept three girls behind to speak to them about their mean remarks to her daughter Mellie who has fled in tears to the corridor lavatory. Since they had been laughing at Mellie's purple stained facial birthmark, Rose felt compelled to chide them about bullying. The ensuing plot revolves around Rose's split-second decision: does she lead the three little girls sitting in front of her to safety outdoors or does she follow Mellie down the hall to the girls' room? Both Mellie and one of her tormentors will be seriously injured and there will be speculation as to whether Rose is a heroine or irresponsible in her duties. As an investigation ensues as to the cause of the fire, Rose faces a lawsuit for negligence which wreaks havoc on her life, as well as that of her family. When she decides that her lawyers are not representing her as she wishes, she decides to become pro-active in her own defense, following hunches and suspicions that lead her into very dangerous territory. There is suspense here, as well as surprise, in addition to analysis of legal and ethical issues. At the heart of it all is a mother's deep love and devotion to the safety and well-being of her child.

SUMMER HOUSE WITH SWIMMING POOL
(Translated from Dutch)

by
Herman Koch

"I am a doctor," begins the narrator, Dr. Marc Schlosser, in this most unusual novel of a physician who has an acute antipathy toward the human bodies he examines. In this respect, he reminds me of the misanthropic Jonathan Swift, 18th century author of *Gulliver's Travels*, who also had an aversion to the odors and sights of that "massive, stinking ball of flesh." He seems most disdainful of obese women with their many folds of skin, as well as gay men and their sexual proclivities. This is not a book for the dainty or squeamish who might find his descriptions gross, graphic, and offensive. Nor will the reader find Dr. Schlosser a likeable character since he seems to have no feeling or empathy for his patients -- just pretends to listen to their complaints and dispenses pills easily. Less likeable is the other main character, Ralph Meier, a renowned stage actor, who is his patient. The story actually begins when Ralph invites Marc and his family (wife and two daughters) to Ralph's "summer house with swimming pool." Marc's acceptance of Ralph's hospitality will change all of their lives. Despite the aforementioned negative aspects, this is a compelling tale of human-dynamics, precarious relationships, suspicions and mistrust. There is a spiraling aura of mystery as Marc tries to discover who assaulted his young daughter on the beach, and in a final act of vengeance believes he is achieving retribution.

THE WRONG SIDE OF GOODBYE

by
Michael Connelly

    Private investigator Harry Bosch is busy working on a serial rapist case when he is contacted by 85-year-old Whitney Vance, an extremely wealthy scion descended from a mining family that traces back to the California Gold Rush. Vance has reason to believe that he may have an heir out there somewhere and Harry is hired to find him or her. Between the two simultaneous cases Harry will find himself shifting his attention back and forth. Each is equally pressing since there is a rapist out there waiting to attack another victim, and Vance has reason to believe he may be dying. So begins investigation of the rapist's crime scenes as well as trailing any leads to a possible Vance progeny. The latter will take him back to memories of his own time in Vietnam where Vance's only son was killed, hours of researching that son's past, making inquiries with former Vietnam vets who fought alongside the junior Vance, and following any leads that might unearth a family member to whom the elder Vance wants to bequeath his fortune. But there are greedy business partners and board members of Vance's company who do not want Harry to succeed in his quest and deliberately place obstacles in his way. When Vance suddenly turns up dead, the investigation takes a more serious turn. At the same time, Harry's female partner, on finding the rapist, disappears which makes Harry frantic with both fear and guilt since he sent her alone to check out a location while he focused on finding Vance's heir. There is mystery here as well as suspense; a carefully developed, escalating plot; a few red herrings; an extremely dangerous foe still on the loose -- all the elements of a good mystery.

The author, Michael Connelly, is the author of twenty-eight previous novels, which include *New York Times* "Best-sellers" *The Crossing* and *The Burning Room*.

BREAKING WILD

by
Diane Les Becquets

Breaking Wild is similar to "Best-seller" *Wild* by Cheryl Strayed in that the protagonists in both books are troubled young women in search of a catharsis. In addition, both seek out an arduous, punishing trek through the wilderness to cleanse themselves of the pain and anger that is eating away at them. In this novel, the main character, Amy Raye Latour, is conflict-ridden because although she loves her husband Farrell, she is driven and unable to control her impulsive, destructive behavior. Promiscuous and unfaithful, she is overcome with self-loathing which leads her to run off and disappear for weeks or months at a time. Her guilt is compounded by the fact that when she abandons Farrell, she is also leaving two children that mean the world to her; in fact, she feels that the only redeeming thing in her life is her devoted mothering of these children. Since childhood she has been drawn to natural settings where in shady woods, crystal lakes, and horse pastures she finds calm and peace; and in vast and wild places, she finds excitement and adventure. So from time to time she will seek a solitary place for a spell and let "Nature do the healing." On this occasion, she has chosen to hunt elk in the Colorado mountains accompanied by two men, one of whom is her present lover. Late one night, she goes off on her own, leaving their camp site to track an elk. Having grown up on a farm and skillfully trained to hunt in her youth by her grandfather, she is more than capable and fully equipped for this endeavor and expects that her companions will eventually catch up with her. So begins the odyssey of an arduous and dangerous trip that will result in a search-and-rescue mission; except that after four months in freezing temperatures, subject to hypothermia and frostbite, without food, and beset by cougars and mountain lions, it is not likely that Amy will survive. The author not only focuses on the conflict of "man versus nature" but also on "man versus himself" since

Amy is in much need of "fixing" psychologically. Although she traces part of her problem to an incident with her cousins in the grandparents' barn when she was a youngster, she realizes that in adulthood her bad choices have been her own and that she must assume responsibility for her actions. Suspense builds as the reader wonders whether she will have the chance to correct her mistakes.

SOMEONE

by
Alice McDermott

Winner of the 2013 "National Book Award," Alice McDermott has once again demonstrated her mastery of writing in her latest book *Someone*, a serious and thought-provoking novel about the main character Marie's life experiences and those of her brother Gabe, both growing up in an Irish Catholic family in Brooklyn. It is a study of characters in the truest sense, revealing them subtly and compassionately. Gabe, to whom she has always had a strong bond, forever remains a mystery to Alice. An extremely studious and pious child, he is the "golden boy" in his parents' eyes, while she, mischievous and feisty, is called the "little pagan." Fostered by his parents' encouragement, Gabe enters the seminary; but after less than a year in the priesthood, he returns home. Since his father has died prematurely, he feels it his responsibility to support his mother and sister. But it seems there is more to the loss of his vocation than he reveals. At 17, Alice is also adrift in finding her own place in the world, suffering heartbreak after her own disappointing first love affair and uninterested in finding employment. Eventually, she secures a job with the neighborhood undertaker as his assistant, filling the role of "consoling angel" to the bereaved, as well as organizing wakes and funerals. In this capacity, she becomes privy to the hidden pasts and secrets of the various deceased which allows the reader to become acquainted with other complex characters. Most have suffered in some way: the young man home from the war, left blind from the gassing, and wallowing in depression and loneliness; the lame "gimp" who befriends him since they are both handicapped in some manner; the homely, clumsy young girl who dreams of romance but dies falling down her own stairs; Alice's own tortured brother; and finally, the insecure and garrulous orphaned veteran who becomes her beloved and protective husband. All have their own stories which are revealed to us skillfully, often in flashback. There is pain here, adversity, yearning, sorrow, loss -- all conveyed through recollections of her old neighborhood and its residents. Although blind by the end the book, the author remembers all her experiences with vivid clarity -- her budding teenage sexuality, the agonizing and nearly fatal birth of her first child, her nightmarish dreams, her brother's struggle for sanity. McDermott's writing is so superb that the reader is there in each of these moments with Marie as the story unfolds seamlessly.

ORPHAN # 8

by
Kim van Alkemade

The main character, Rachel Rabinowitz (aka "Orphan #8"), is a nurse at a Jewish home for the elderly when she is assigned a female patient, Dr. Mildred Solomon. Despite the fact that Mildred is extremely frail and desiccated by the final stages of a disease to which she will soon succumb, Rachel recognizes the old woman as the physician who subjected her to radiation as part of a study at the orphanage where Rachel grew up following the death of her mother at the hands of her father. Upon seeing Dr. Solomon, Rachel is overwhelmed with multiple ambivalent emotions since the experiments caused Rachel irreparable harm. First, she developed alopecia which left her bald, affecting her self-esteem and self-image her entire life. Recently she has been diagnosed with breast cancer, another result of the radiation to which she was exposed as a child. Rachel has endured an extremely difficult life -- first, the shocking loss of both parents; then separation from her beloved older brother; many days at the home in isolation, restricted confinement for exposure to various illnesses; complete lack of attention and nurturing throughout her formative years. Hers has been a lonely and sad existence. When Rachel summons courage to confront Dr. Solomon with the harm for which she was responsible, to Rachel's astonishment, Dr. Solomon is neither remorseful nor apologetic, defending her actions in the name of scientific research. Rachel is not only angry, but also overcome with a desire for revenge. She is in a position to take it since she is in charge of Dr. Solomon's morphine doses. There is a lot of inner turmoil and conflict with which Rachel struggles in this novel. As the reader follows her harrowing situation, as well as her frantic search out West to locate her brother, it is impossible not to feel compassion for this innocent child's plight, as well as outrage for the young Dr. Solomon's careless disregard for the research subjects whom she consciously exploited to advance her own career. I will leave it to the reader to find out how Rachel resolves her dilemma. Will she wreak vengeance for the personal damage caused by Dr. Solomon or will compassion and forgiveness prevail?

A FIREPROOF HOME FOR THE BRIDE

by
Amy Scheibe

Set in the Midwest in the 1950s, *A Fireproof Home for the Bride* is the story of 18-year-old Emmaline Nelson, the eldest daughter of a Lutheran farming family. Her pious, ultra-traditional and secretive mother encourages her to accept the attentions of a wealthy neighbor boy Ambrose to whom Emmy was betrothed as a child. They have grown up together as playmates, and she feels she knows all there is to know about him. However, under the influence of an intimidating racist Mr. Davidson, whom Ambrose greatly admires, he has become a disciple of a group similar to the Ku Klux Klan. At the same time Emmy has become the object of attention of an Irish Catholic boy, Bobby Doyle, whom her mother forbids her to see. Both boys exert immense pressure on her, and eventually she becomes the victim of a date rape. In the background is Emmy's sweet and innocent younger sister Birdie who becomes Ambrose's love interest once he is rejected by Emmy, which puts Birdie in danger. As Emmy is trying to sort out what SHE wants rather than what others want her to do, she rejects the option of marrying so young and limiting her life to that of a rural country wife and mother. Her guidance counselor and aunt, who recognize her potential, encourage her to attend college and seek a career. In order to earn money toward that goal, she takes a job in a movie theater owned by a Jewish immigrant, as well as a job at a newspaper, where she encounters an enlightened young man who treats her with respect and acknowledges her abilities. At this point the story picks up. The theater is burned as a result of arson. Her grandmother makes some intriguing, cryptic remarks on her death bed which lead Emmy to a search among the piles of boxes, trunks, and other family letters and birth certificates in the attic. Much of it puzzles her as some of the diaries and records kept by her grandfather appear to be in code. With the help of the reporter with whom she works, together they begin to solve long-hidden secrets about her family. Many have lived lies for years and refused to acknowledge them. One was a member of the KKK involved in violent crimes; some were involved in romances and affairs that produced offspring that share a kinship other than what Emmy has been led to believe all these years. Although the book starts slowly, at the end there is a lot of action, including assault, abuse, pregnancy, kidnapping, drugging, arson, prejudice-based violence, and the like. Parts are difficult to follow, particularly the biological relationships between some of the characters since at the beginning Emmy and the reader had been unaware of the family's deceit. Although the book is rather lengthy and requires attention to details, *People* magazine recommended it in a recent issue which led me to select it for review.

HAPPY PEOPLE READ AND DRINK COFFEE

by
Agnes Martin-Lugand

Proprietor of a French bookstore named Happy People, Diane is bereft, having lost both her beloved young husband and cherished little girl in a car accident. She has withdrawn from the world and languishes in grief, remaining in bed for days, wrapped in her husband's shirt. Despite the encouragement of her parents and a dear friend Felix, she refuses to get on with her life, feeling she no longer has anything to live for. In an attempt to be left in peace, she suddenly decides to leave all that she has known and rent a cottage in an unknown town named Mulranny. Here she hopes to find healing or, at least, respite from all the painful memories of home. Instead she finds a windswept, rainy, rugged coastal village, as well as a rude, obnoxious neighbor Edward, the son of her landlords, Abbie and Jack. This couple and their daughter Judith, on the other hand, are warm and welcoming. She will endure many angry run-ins with Edward who has his own history of loss and disappointment; both remain stand-offish, concealing their grief and pain. Eventually each will soften as they try to deny a growing attachment to each other. But all does not proceed smoothly, as Megan, Edward's former girlfriend, shows up just as Diane and Edward are drifting into a warm relationship. An "International Best-seller," *Happy People…* has been translated from French into English, as well as other languages. It is a story about tragedy and loss as the mourner struggles to let go of the past and come to terms with present reality. Written by a former clinical psychologist, Agnes Martin-Lugand is in a position to know about coping with bereavement and the resulting emotions, particularly a spouse's ambivalence and guilt in starting a new relationship.

THE WOMAN UPSTAIRS

by
Claire Messud

A psychological study of an unfulfilled 42-year-old spinster Nora Eldridge, *The Woman Upstairs* focuses on the anger, disappointment and rage that consume this middle-aged third grade teacher. Nora feels that she and her life are of little consequence and substance. Regretful of all the years wasted being the dutiful daughter, straight "A" student, good worker, favorite teacher, she feels trapped in a boring, uneventful existence in which the arrival of the latest catalogue is the highlight of her day. With immense personal disdain, she describes herself as "the woman upstairs who smiles brightly, never makes a sound, living in quiet desperation behind closed doors." Beneath this calm facade is a female ready to burst with internal conflict and intense yearnings. In fact, the novel begins with a tirade replete with shocking expletives and invective so incongruous to the genial lady Nora appears to be. Until one day she meets the parents of her young student, Reza Shabid, in whom she has taken a particular interest. She delights in the child's shiny black curls that curve sweetly around the nape of his neck, causing the reader to wonder why she is so drawn to this boy. Might it be that she yearns for a child of her own? And more intriguing is the relationship she seeks with Reza's mother Sirena, a charming and elegant Italian artist. Once Nora herself had been an aspiring artist when as a young girl, her parents insisted that she forgo attending art school to pursue teaching as a more practical career. Her mother forced her to promise that she would become self-sufficient, never dependent on a man for every measly dime to be doled out. Eventually she will share a studio loft with Sirena, and the author vaguely hints at a sexual attraction; but Nora is equally drawn to Sirena's handsome husband Skandar, a Lebanese professor at Harvard. When the entire Shabid family abruptly leaves Boston to return to their native land, Nora is deeply hurt and puzzled since all three had become close, and the Shabids left no notice or message regarding their departure. Eventually they will return, but something unsettling has been brewing within Nora since their arrival into her life. Nora will insist to her closest confidant that her attraction to Sirena is not sexual; rather she inspires Nora as an artist, makes her laugh and feel alive. But in truth, Nora herself cannot identify the myriad emotions all in the Shabid family evoke in her. When she begins to babysit Reza, she likes to think of herself as his mother, which seems to be stepping beyond reasonable bounds. In addition, she indulges in fantasy, dreaming of having an affair with Skandar or imagining all four of them as a family. This may be a case for a therapist, but first to be addressed is Nora's frustrating sense of invisibility, resentful of being "unthanked, unacknowledged, and unadmired, always needing to cede, swerve, and step aside."

Read to find out how this unusual relationship unweaves and how Nora handles her puzzling feelings regarding the Shabids.

FAMILY PICTURES

by
Jane Green

Sylvie - a happily married devoted wife, homemaker and mother of Eve. Laid-back, sweet, trusting, unassuming, she lives in a modest house in California -- cozy, inviting, and comfortable. Much of her time is consumed with a teenage daughter struggling with anorexia and bulimia as well as an aging, difficult mother.

Maggie -- a perfectly coiffed, tanned, couturier-dressed socialite and pillar of the community; attractive wife and mother of three: Grace, Chris, and Buck, all of whom live in an ostentatious, perfectly decorated, mansion-like home in Connecticut.

Although their lifestyles are very different, these two women share something in common; a husband who travels frequently on business and is rarely at home. Both will be forced to confront the same shocking, life-shattering experience which will turn their lives upside-down when Sylvie's daughter Eve befriends Maggie's daughter Grace. This connection will unearth secrets and bring both families together. Although on the surface, Sylvie and Maggie appear to be made of different cloth, both will be tested to the limit of their endurance, resilience, and strength in holding their families together. This is a story of betrayal and disloyalty. It is also a story of what constitutes character and how unexpected adversity can often lead a person to reassess her priorities and the direction of her life.

SIRACUSA

by
Delia Ephron

A darkly intriguing novel, *Siracusa* revolves around two couples, Michael and Lizzie, who are on vacation with Finn, Taylor, and their precocious 10-year-old daughter Snow. It soon becomes apparent that Lizzie has arranged this "double-date" trip to be with Finn with whom she has a history. Both marriages are troubled, fragile, and falling apart; and all four seem engaged in a power struggle of sorts.

At one point, one of the characters wonders, "How the hell did we end up with the wrong people?" There is flirting, suspicion, hostility, resentment, and secrets -- all of which the strange, uncommunicative Snow observes "like wallpaper in the background as if she'd perfected the art of invisibility." As this odd child is taking it all in, it is she who will become the catalyst for the surprising, unexpected twist at the end.

Each of the individuals has his/her motive for taking this excursion: the insecure and controlling Taylor relishes the opportunity to be in proximity to the famous and successful novelist Michael, as if he gives her cachè. An extremely neurotic mother, she is intent on giving her elusive, emotionally distant daughter lessons on ancient history and antiquity. Her efforts are "over-the-top" and obsessive. She seems "to have no idea where she ends and Snow begins."

The peculiar Snow seems to enjoy the attention that Michael gives her, if even in a seductive and inappropriate manner. Michael, for his part, seems to be picking up pieces of this trip and these characters for a novel he has been struggling to finish due to writer's block. Lizzie appears in competition with him since she is a journalist who envies his success. Finn, who just seems along for the ride, insists that Michael is a fraud, as well as a skunk. First, he points out that much of Michael's background, such as having gone to Yale, is made up; also since Finn cares for Lizzie, he hates that Michael is deceiving her with a young girl named Kathy. When Kathy appears, her arrival will set in motion a bizarre series of irrevocable events that will direly affect all the participants, none more than the unfathomable Snow.

Ephron builds the suspense gradually as she combs the mysteries of marriages, the tensions, the betrayals, the ennui, the financial considerations, the sexual attraction to others, the personal incompatibilities. This is all as she is negotiating a gripping plot. You may not like individuals that populate her book since they reveal some extremely unappealing and narcissistic traits, but they sustain your interest in a compelling manner right up to the jarring conclusion.

An added strength is Ephron's ability to convey the local color of an Italian island in her sensory description of the locale and the food: the "ropey spaghetti… tousled with tiny clams, baby tomatoes, parsley, and showered in toasted bread crumbs." Earlier in Rome at the Trevi Fountain in all its glory: "a turbulent, crazy fantasy… exquisite naked marble men frolicking with winged horses, the god of the sea Oceanus… naked too except for a swirling cloak, his body muscled in perfection… the waterfalls obliterating all sound." At dinner "grilled artichokes, *fritti* of all sorts to be shared, forks colliding in excitement, zucchini flowers voted best… the setting a candlelit patio cloistered between crumbling architectural survivors in a humbler part of Rome." The author's vivid description, in and of itself, is an invitation to the book.

A TREE GROWS IN BROOKLYN

by
Betty Smith

Unlike most of the reviews here, *A Tree Grows in Brooklyn* is not recent, but it was new to me. I can't imagine that for so avid a reader as I, somehow I missed this book -- so TRUE, so FINE, so INSPIRING, so SUBLIME and UNIVERSAL in scope and theme, as to surpass all current works. This was a book I could not put down and did not want to end, which is really one criteria of a GREAT work. It is a life-affirming novel of 11-year-old Francie Nolan growing up in a Brooklyn tenement in 1912. She is a most perceptive and precocious child trying to understand her family and the world she inhabits. There is her lovingly charming but weak dad, an alcoholic; her practical and steely mother determined not only to keep the family afloat but also to see that her children escape this grinding poverty through education. Francie is a born writer who narrates her experiences and expresses her feelings in the most expressive and exquisitely nuanced prose. As she moves from wide-eyed childhood innocence to more mature adolescence, she begins to better comprehend the reality of her world -- her relatives and neighbors, forever struggling to survive from day to day; her better comprehension of her father's addiction and his inability to support the family; the limitations of her drab, dingy, and dismal environment; her disappointment that, try as she might to excel in her studies, it is not likely that she will ever go to college, her sole dream and ambition. In many respects this book is autobiographical, since the author Betty Smith actually lived Francie's difficult life and dreamed Francie's dreams. Smith wrote about her own life as she lived it -- and what SUPERB writing. In addition, there is so much SUBSTANCE here -- simultaneously Smith develops the themes of family connections, separation of class, exploitation of laborers, education of the poor, discrimination against women, the pressures of marriage, hope and disillusion, poverty and its degradation of the soul --

all the drama of people's lives. Portrayed are intensely emotional scenes depicted vividly from this extraordinary child's point of view. Her philosophical musings are far beyond her years as at some point she wonders if this is all that constitutes life -- waking at dawn to go to a toilsome job; putting in hours of mind-dulling and physically exhausting routine; crawling home fatigued to a meager supper which only provides enough sustenance to begin the endless, never-ending cycle again until dying suddenly one day in the same place one was born.

    I came across this title when reading about books sent by the government to US soldiers overseas in WW II to assist with morale. This was the most popular title requested by GIs who read it in the trenches, in camps, even on boats as combatants waiting to be dropped on the shores of Normandy on D-Day. One soldier said he carried his copy through all four years of his deployment and returned with it to the US; it was so precious to him. As a result, I HAD TO KNOW the book that inspired and deeply affected so many. And now I know why. This is a masterpiece of humanity and its fragility; it is an achingly tender portrait of a family, emotionally compelling and REAL. Smith's creation of heart-wrenching, unforgettable characters and her ability to recreate the rich atmosphere of an earlier time and place is testament to her amazing art and talent. This is one book TOO GOOD TO MISS!

IN THE SHADOW OF ALABAMA

by
Judy Reene Singer

For her entire life, Rachel has known a father (Martin Fleischer) who was perpetually angry, volatile, frustrated, and tense. Now he lies in a hospital in need of a surgery when she is summoned to his bedside. She resists going since her sister Sandra, the favored daughter, is with her parents, and Rachel's relationship with her mother is little better than with her father. When her dad succumbs, an unknown black woman appears at the funeral with an apology from her own father (Willie) who once called Rachel's dad a "murderer." This shocks Rachel, although her mother seems less perturbed, and will lead to a visit to Willie to gain answers to his charge. So begins a well-plotted story regarding her father's work in the 1940s as a supervisor at an air force base in Alabama. Willie was one of a crew of a dozen black men, a squadron under Sergeant Fleisher, a Jew whose assignment was to thoroughly maintain and wash planes after each flight. Not only is this a true story based on the author's father's experiences, but it is also enlightening as to the prejudicial treatment of minorities in the deep South at that time. Fleischer is a sharp engineer relegated to "wash duty" only because of race. Willie, also with some engineering background, becomes his best friend and together they work on figuring out why so many planes crash despite being thoroughly checked. Their work is hazardous as they use potent chemicals which burn their skin and sear their lungs. When Fleischer, through weeks and weeks of mathematical calculations and collection of data, finally finds the answer to the puzzle of the plane crashes and brings it to the attention of his superior, racial bigotry rears its ugly head in the worst way possible. Singer paints a sad and tragic picture of the despicable treatment of blacks and Jews not only in this area of the country, but also in the military. From Willie, Rachel will get the answers to why the father she knew was such a broken and damaged man. This is a well-wrought tale that will spark the reader's sense of justice and fairness; it is a story of friendship, betrayal, and trauma that will help in Rachel reaching a better understanding of why her father was the way he was.

THE LANGUAGE OF FLOWERS

by
Vanessa Diffenbaugh

Lily-of-the valley (return to happiness). Orange tiger lily (majesty). Daffodils (new beginnings). Hyacinth (forgiveness). Hazel (reconciliation). Rhododendron (beware!) Jonquil (desire). Starwort or stellaria (welcome). These comprise the language of flowers, as well as other blooms that symbolize a myriad of emotions. Such is the silent type of language used by an angry, remote, quick-tempered young girl named Victoria who has been placed in thirty-two homes or facilities for children in foster care. In most she has been treated poorly, severely punished for disobedience and recalcitrance. The one constant in her life has been Meredith, her caseworker, who for some unknown reason has never given up on her. After repeated rejections, Victoria is finally placed with Elizabeth who is eager to love and nurture her and on Victoria's first visit to her home, spreads a bountiful lunch garnished with starworts -- "welcome to my home and into my life." With Elizabeth, Victoria finally begins to feel loved and understood and also begins to learn about the intrinsic messages of various flowers. For every slow step forward, there are often two steps backward; for Victoria is a severely damaged child. Both look forward to the end of a trial year when Elizabeth can finally officially adopt Victoria. They excitedly anticipate it for months, planning this special milestone, shopping for just the right dress; and when Victoria dons it in a store dressing room, Elizabeth is so overcome with love and joy that she envelopes Victoria in her arms declaring how much she treasures her. Then arrives the day for their courtroom appearance to make the adoption official. Victoria, more excited and happier than she has ever been in her life, dresses in her beautiful outfit and enters Elizabeth's room to model for her, but Elizabeth is unable to stir from her bed. Read this poignant and heart-breaking story to learn the cause of Elizabeth's inability to follow through with her commitment to Victoria. Like the child, you will experience anger, disappointment, shock, and bewilderment as Elizabeth begins to describe her own dysfunctional background with a mother who, like Victoria's, "didn't love her either." This novel is as much a description of our foster care system, which is in dire need of reform, as it is about the "language of flowers."

NON-FICTION

LEGENDS OF THE WEST
Narrative of My Captivity Among the Sioux Indians

by
Fanny Kelly

An avid reader of American Western history, I was fascinated by this compelling narrative of pioneer Fanny Kelly who was captured in Wyoming in 1864 by a band of Oglala Sioux warriors and held captive for many months. In vivid detail, she describes her life among this tribe, replete with both physical and emotional trials and tribulations that would have caused the quick demise of a more delicate and fragile woman. The horrors and deprivations she suffered make riveting reading. Not only does she record her myriad thoughts and feelings in captivity, but also graphically describes her harrowing experiences and the brutality she witnessed. Given what she endured -- first the violent assault on her family, followed by the excruciating abandonment of her child, and days of endless forced riding on horseback across plains and mountains without food or water, crossing violently swirling streams, and the eventual arrival at the hostile Indian encampment in the isolated wilderness -- it is amazing that she retained her sanity. This is **real** drama that actually happened as part of the ongoing battle between the native American Indians and the settlers who coveted their lands and were encouraged by the US government to make their claims as part of Western expansion. Kelly is a talented writer, who despite her terror and imprisonment among ferocious savages, remains keenly aware of the natural beauties of the landscape, even while forced on this grueling journey westward. The prairies over which she travels are covered with waving grass beneath immense deeply blue skies in which flocks of birds with beautiful plumage alight; gurgling, crystal clear brooks offer icy thirst-quenching water; valleys with blooming wildflowers of all varieties afford delightful sprays of color; majestic mountain peaks and bluffs soar upward toward limitless skies. With equal detail, she describes the shock of seeing, dangling from a warrior's lance, what she believes to be the blond scalp of her small daughter with its silken fine hairs. Equally appalling is the chief's necklace fashioned from human finger bones boiled to remove the flesh and used for a game of fun, as we would use tokens for a board game.

Read to find out how Fannie fared following her yo-yo existence, fluctuating from a valued member of the tribe who had a talent for treating wounds to a woman whose life was imperiled by the desire for revenge each time her captors lost members in skirmishes with US cavalry. Hers is a "captivating" (forgive the pun) and tense historic tale that she fortunately lived to tell. Her day-by-day account of her time among these native-Americans – their customs, beliefs, attire, rituals, etc, -- is a recording of the history of these indigenous people.

SPINSTER
Making a Life of One's Own

By
Kate Bolick

A spinster by choice, Kate Bolick has researched the growing numbers of women who, like herself, prefer to remain unmarried. In the United States today, single Americans outnumber marrieds. For her, not marrying has been a conflict-ridden decision following years of personal turmoil and angst. In part, she attributes her decision to remain unattached to the writings of four females whose works have had a profound influence upon her thinking: poet Edna St. Vincent Millay, essayist Maeve Brennan, columnist Neith Boyce, and novelist Edith Wharton -- all of whom shared an ambivalence to the institution of marriage. On one extreme side of the spectrum is another writer Doris Lessing who goes so far as to call it "a prison we choose to live inside." Another exults in "the extravagant pleasure" of simply being by herself. Realizing that some would consider such an attitude selfish, Bolick concedes that many others follow the traditional path: complete school, leave home, start a career, get married, and have children. Although she quotes a 1962 poll that indicated the majority of wives said they were happy with their conformity to this pattern, only 10% wanted their daughters to follow suit. Their advice was "to go to college; wait a little longer; live a little first."

The first author whose ideas Bolick found appealing was Maeve Brennan (mentioned above) whose desire "to be alone" resonated with her since Bolick suspects she herself has always harbored the "spinster wish" as early as her twenties. Bolick finds Brennan the first author who writes about <u>herself, not in relation to someone else</u> -- whether lover, husband, child, or parent. In one of Brennan's stories, a woman, probably Maeve herself, is sitting alone in a crowded New York City restaurant amidst the bustle and chatter of other people's lives -- reading, taking a sip of coffee, oblivious of the bedlam and noise surrounding her both inside and outside. "<u>This</u>," Bolick thinks, "is what I want for myself," but this desire also frightens her since the single woman has always been an anomaly; and the very word <u>spinster</u> has always had a derogatory connotation. " What does this mean if she craves such an existence?" she asks herself.

Over the years, Bolick has had many relationships with men -- even fallen in love with some -- but she says, "I was most alive when alone." She completely identifies with Neith Boyce (mentioned previously) who in her *Memoirs* describes her feelings upon landing an editing job she relishes. Boyce even delights in the daily commute to work, the brisk walk, the people rushing in and out of the subway, even the worn, dirty stone steps to the office. Though she lives in a rather squalid one room flat looking on a backyard of weeds, clothing flapping on the clothes-lines, she emphasizes it was "all my own and my complete independence was enough. How I enjoyed it!" Bollick wants to be Boyce.

Another influence is the poet Edna St. Vincent Millay, a libertine free spirit who wrote erotic verse. She considered marriage "a hideous state of bondage" and lived an unconventional life on her own terms.

Last she devotes a chapter to Charlotte Perkins Gilman who in 1892 wrote a shocking short story "The Yellow Wall-paper," published in *The New England Magazine*. This narrative seems to be a warning to creative and strong-willed women of the dire results of trying to suppress those traits. Perkins, a Rhode Islander, attended The Rhode Island School of Design. In 1878 she founded the Sanitary Gymnasium for Ladies and Children, a women's fitness center in Providence. Although she vowed never to marry, in 1884 she did just that and, after giving birth to a daughter, went into a deep depression. Eventually she divorced her husband and abandoned her family to develop a "cooperative housekeeping movement" in which women were encouraged to join together to form housekeeping collaboratives and be reimbursed by their husbands who benefitted from their work. Rhode Island has always had free thinkers, beginning with Roger Williams, so, I suppose Charlotte Perkins, was not the first.

Books that Transport to Other Places

In my opinion, this book reveals a woman, Kate Bollick, who has been struggling with her inclination to live life as she wishes, although the problem seems to be that she doesn't quite know what it is she wants. At times, she desires male companionship but seems phobic of commitment. She yearns for independence but then creeps back to her parental homestead when overwhelmed. At the end of the book she seems somewhat comfortable with her choice to remain single, but it seems the entire book writing experience was a search to find other authors whose own opinions would provide confirmation of her choice. So, I ask, is it really her own decision?

Note: This is not a book for light summer reading. It is replete with quotes by famous female writers philosophizing about the institution of marriage, and questions regarding how females can live authentically and realize their full potential without the constraints of cultural mores. Nevertheless, it is a well-researched and intriguing subject. It seems that a valid question for some women would be:

"Tell me, what is it you plan to do

With your one wild and precious life?"

(from poem "The Summer Day" by Mary Oliver, a friend of Edna St. Vincent Millay's sister and who lived at the Millay estate after Edna died).

THE BLACK HAND
*The Epic War Between a Brilliant Detective
& the Deadliest Secret Society in America*

by
Stephan Talty

Fascinating! Intriguing! Suspenseful! "The Black Hand" refers to one of the deadliest terrorist organizations to ever blight the American landscape. Starting in 1903, a group of barbaric and ruthless criminals, many of whom emigrated from Sicily to America, began to prey on their fellow Italian immigrants who became the victims of kidnapping, extortion, bombing, and murder. The majority of Italian immigrants living in New York City ghettos were subjected to threats and intimidation causing many to flee back to their homeland to escape persecution. Left unchecked, more Black Hand societies began cropping up in states across America spreading fear, destruction, and death. Children were kidnapped for ransom and later found dead and stuffed in chimneys. Businesses were blown up. Only one man, Detective Giuseppe Petrosino, an immigrant himself, was bold and courageous enough to make it his life mission to eradicate these thugs and their diabolical acts. Petrosino was brilliant in his tactics and use of disguises; posing as a grignono (greenhorn), he managed to infiltrate their groups. His most valuable asset was his ability to "memorize every detail … names of thousands of Italian criminals, their faces, vital statistics, regional background, habits, and crimes." Early in his career, Petrosino had become friends with Teddy Roosevelt who later said of the wily detective, "He didn't know the name of fear." Despite his devotion to ridding this country of these villains, he was often rebuffed by his Irish superiors in the NYPD who not only refused his requests for additional men, but also went out of their way to thwart his efforts to arrest and deport these malefactors. But his countrymen sought him out when they were victimized; and his bravery and cunning became legendary. Eventually, he headed what became known as "The Italian Squad, a little band of zealots" whose success in rooting out these notorious undesirables earned Manhattan's admiration and trust. But for every Black-Hander they caught, more and more entered the US daily so that it became an overwhelming and never-ending game of cat-and-mouse. With amazing foresight and instinct, Petrosino had even warned Pres. McKinley that he was a likely target for assassination from a group of anarchists responsible for the murder of the Italy's King Umberto I, which was exactly how McKinley met his end

Read about this "lone" hero (referred to as "the Italian Sherlock Holmes") whose deep love of his newly adopted country, the USA, caused him to endanger himself and devote his life to protecting his countrymen from persecution. Much of the book reads like a compelling and dramatic thriller with evil villains, beleaguered victims, and violent crimes against humanity; however, it is all true and factual.

It is amazing that little has been written about this "lion" who championed the rights of his persecuted compatriots. Thousands came to pay tribute at his funeral, one declaring "Joe saved my life;" another "I'd be a dead man but for Joe." 250,000 mourners, more than had gathered for Pres. McKinley's funeral, thronged the streets in Manhattan to pay him homage. Even the later funeral of Rudolph Valentino, America's most famous actor, did not draw such crowds. Petrosino was cut down in Sicily still doing his job, diligently tracking down the names of gangsters previously prosecuted in Italy so that they would be prevented from entering the US under an immigration provision he had been responsible for bringing to fruition. In every sense, he was a "savior" of his people.

WHEN BOOKS WENT TO WAR
The Stories That Helped Us Win World War II

by
Molly Guptill Manning

On May 10, 1933, thousands of students in Berlin were joined by 40,000 spectators to partake in the mass burning of millions of books deemed offensive to the German state. These bonfires spread throughout the country; and after the extermination of books, began the extermination of people, primarily Jews, in an effort to "purify" the nation. As this continued and escalated throughout Eastern Europe, it became obvious that Hitler was a danger to democracy. However, Americans, as well as their President Franklin D. Roosevelt, were reluctant to become involved. Nevertheless, the US War Department began to prepare by building military training camps. Not only were they initially dirty, stinking, muddy "hell holes," but also totally inadequate -- six to eight men slept in 16' x 16' tents where sparks from the single stove for heating burned holes in the flimsy tent material which required dousing all night. Moreover, they did not have guns, essential equipment, or any means of diversion after the many hours of grueling drills and exhausting exercises. One group, The American Library Association, began a campaign to collect books for men in uniform. Once America entered the war and men were shipped overseas, the demand for light-weight paperbacks was so intense that the government began to publish The Armed Services Editions (ASE). Over the course of the war, ASE shored up weary, exhausted, and disillusioned soldiers. These books were read in foxholes, waiting in line for chow or a haircut, even in the hours before American GIs stormed the beaches of Normandy and crossed the Rhine. ASEs and letters from home were the most treasured items. Some carried their books around in snow, rain, mud, and combat. One soldier, Charles Bolte, hospitalized in South Africa and facing amputation of his leg, was given a copy of an Ernest Hemingway book in which the hero found that crying eased the pain. Until then, Bolte had never dared cry. "It helped me," said Bolte, who endured multiple surgeries. He asserted that the dozens of books he read during this time assisted him in his recovery. Tens of thousands would experience the same therapeutic effects. Another wrote: "I want to thank you profoundly for the men in this God-forsaken part of the globe. All we have for recreation is a ping-pong set with one paddle. Last week we received your book which I read one night around the campfire. The men howled. I have not heard such laughs in months."

The most popular was Betty Smith's *A Tree Grows in Brooklyn* (reviewed here) that was so vivid an account of childhood to make many men feel as though she was writing about their own -- allowing them "to live their lives all over again."

The Southern writer Katherine Ann Porter's short stories also earned wide appeal because she so "delicately exposed private, deeply personal experiences and emotions giving the reader the impression that she understood his innermost thoughts and feelings." Some wrote to her about relating to a certain character, others about feeling a layer of loneliness "stripped away" as they read her prose. Some even expressed emotions in letters to this author which they kept hidden in those sent to their families. One soldier kept his collection all through the war and brought it home with him. He said he never tired of reading it again and again; it so comforted him.

In addition, Rosemary Taylor's *A Chicken for Every Sunday*, a surprise favorite among the men, focused on an adolescent girl whose mother runs a busy boarding house. The narrator not only gives an amusing account of the experience, but also describes a long list of zany characters who are served scrumptious dinners every night. One GI said it gave him a "refreshing sense of a wholesome way of life left temporarily behind" to which he was eager to return.

The comments of these soldiers are testimony to the comfort and enjoyment the ASE provided. Even those stationed on remote islands in the Pacific could count on their weekly rations of books. "You wouldn't take our books away, would you?" queried one GI of Lt. Col. Trautman, who recognized that "their appetite for ASE's was insatiable."

After the war, other types of books were needed. ASE had served its purpose, and soldiers returning home turned their sights to earning a living. As a result, libraries across the country focused on helping them learn more about the GI Bill of Rights which enabled many to enroll in college. *The Story of Penicillin, Miracles of Military Medicine,* and *Burma Surgeon* inspired those interested in a medical career. John Wharton's *The Theory and Practice of Earning a Living* was of interest to more business-minded individuals. Bellamy Partridge's *Country Lawyer* romanticized small town law practice, while John Floherty's *Inside the FBI* provided information on that organization. Author Oliver Gramlings *AP: The Story of News* appealed to those interested in journalism.

The types of books changed, but there is no doubt about their value in lifting the spirits and providing escape and mental stimulation to those suffering loneliness, ennui, physical discomfit, danger, anxiety, and the traumatic loss of normalcy. One Marine hospitalized, while malaria ravaged his body, wrote that his ASE edition of *A Tree Grows in Brooklyn* allowed him to feel again. "Ever since I carried a stretcher from which my buddy's life dripped away in precious blood ... I have felt hard and cynical ... no longer capable of loving anything or anybody. I existed with 'a dead heart' and 'a dulled mind' --- unable to feel anything. But as I read this book, something inside me began to stir, my heart turned over and I became alive again ... I am a battle-hardened Marine... and I'm not ashamed to say I wept over a piece of fiction."

Hitler and the Nazis tried to eradicate the power of words by destroying books, but ironically the ASE's were powerful weapons in sustaining the spirits of those who became victorious. *When Books Went to War* is one inspiring book about an extraordinary program that was indispensable in sustaining the morale of American troops during WWII ... "it is the story of pens that were as mighty as swords."

NB: Other highly popular ASEs

Sea Wolf (Jack London)

White Fang (Jack London)

Call of the Wild (Jack London)

Candide (Voltaire)

The Time Machine (H. G. Wells)

War of the Worlds (H. G. Wells)

America (Stephen Vincent Benet)

The Great Gatsby by F. Scott Fitzgerald, written in 1925, was considered a failure during the author's life. However, it became a favorite when printed as an ASE in October 1945. The GI's praise for it caused it to become an American literary classic.

PROOF OF HEAVEN

by
Eben Alexander, MD

"I was blind, but now I see."

Fascinating! Intriguing! Thought-provoking! Such is the book by the renowned neuro-surgeon Eben Alexander. In 2008 at the age of 54, Dr. Alexander developed a rare meningitis-type illness that attacked his brain, leaving him in a coma for seven days. The prognosis was grim -- actually hopeless. No one had ever survived this illness following so long a period of unconsciousness. As the bacteria devoured his cortex, he entered an unfamiliar world of "indescribable beauty radiating fine filaments of white-gold light -- brilliant, vibrant, stunning." There he encountered "higher beings," one in particular, a female dressed in blue who ushered him through this realm. Up until this point, Dr. Alexander had never given credence to descriptions of NDE (near-death-experiences) described by his own patients and others; he had been skeptical. His work had always been based on scientific and empirical evidence. Read to find out why Dr. Alexander so strongly asserts that he met the Divine Source -- despite the fact that, prior to this, he had never been an overly-religious man. And even more surprising, read to learn who he believes escorted him through this higher universe -- an earlier deceased relative of whom he was totally unaware. More than anything else, this book is a prime example of the well-known words: "I was blind, but now I see."

AVIATRIX
First Woman Pilot for Hughes Airwest

by
Mary Bush Shipko

Mary Bush Shipko was one of those women who "broke glass ceilings" before the expression became popular. Trained while a youngster in the cockpit of her father's planes on his 100 acre airport in Dania, Florida, she became familiar with all aspects of flight. Her flying lessons began in the 1960s and from them, she developed a sense of fun, exhilaration, freedom, and joy that never subsided throughout her life time. She became knowledgeable and meticulous regarding pre-flight procedures -- walking around the plane and observing all mechanisms, using checklists to start the engine, contacting ground control to receive taxi instructions, and checking the instrument panel, as well as weather and airport information. Once airborne, she would practice take-offs, other maneuvers, and landings because her dad emphasized that skill, knowledge, and determination were only part of the equation. She had to devote many hours to develop real flying skills, in addition to familiarizing herself with routes, navigational aids, and the workings of various airports. Mary diligently applied herself to all of it. After completing college, she took her test for a private pilot's license on a Beechcraft D-18, a rather difficult "bird," and passed with flying colors. It was also that design on which she earned her commercial license in 1973; and on other types of aircraft (including old military planes), earned her multi-engine license, transport pilot's license, seaplane license, in addition to passing requirements as a Certified Flight Instructor -- no small achievements. For some years she flew transports from Florida to the Bahamas, Jamaica, Columbia, Mexico, Panama, Belize, Guatemala, etc. However, her goal was to become a full-fledged commercial pilot flying passenger planes. She achieved that dream when hired by Hughes Airwest (owned by the famous Howard Hughes) to fly DC-3s, 6s, 7s and 9s. She was also adept at flying the Fairchild F-27 and B-727. Although fully qualified and exceptionally skilled with handling all of these different planes, Mary soon ran into other types of turbulence unrelated to the air. Even when she out-performed other pilots (and perhaps because of it), she would get suggestive comments: "That was a really great landing. I bet you're good at other things too," and some would graphically specify what they meant. Today it would be called sexual harassment, although it was not openly recognized at that time. In fact, when she attempted to bring it to a superior's attention, he declared that such a thing did "not exist" and whatever "discomfit" she was experiencing should be "sucked-up" as part of the job. It had first begun with her flying partner suggesting "isometric breast exercises to help with her problem." Later an extremely pornographic picture was tossed in her lap as she took the co-pilot's seat, and another asked her to report to his hotel bedroom regarding an error she had made. Of course, she had made no errors; and when she refused to comply with his advances, he spread gossip that she was a lesbian. It became much more serious when the captain instructed her to assume control of the plane, directed her to manipulate certain controls to dangerously high levels, then left her alone to use the rest room. When the plane began to shudder and shake and he did not return, she realized he had set her up. At the risk of insubordination, she disobeyed his orders and returned the plane to an appropriate altitude. Even simply entering the pilots' lounge, she was subjected to snickering, innuendo, lewd jokes, whisperings of "whore," and general ostracism. They simply "did not want a female in the cockpit." Of course, there were "a few good men" -- gentlemanly pilots who recognized her ability, afforded her the respect she was due, and tolerated her, even if they did not genuinely welcome her presence. Read to find out how this chronic and unwarranted abuse affected her confidence, health, self-esteem, and ultimately her love of flying. I attended an author/book presentation by Mary Bush Shipko, who even now in her 60s, remains a very attractive woman, which may have been part of the problem. I admired her reluctance to openly denigrate those who aimed to ruin her career, leaving the reader to learn in the book about the pain and suffering they caused her. One immediately senses that she is a deeply religious individual who attempted to pray and push on with determination in an attempt to survive and continue working at what she loved to do.

Books that Transport to Other Places

Aviatrix is a very frank and enlightening description of one brave, intelligent, and truly capable woman's experiences in a career dominated by men often known as "sky gods" who truly believed they were.

THE MARRIAGE BUREAU
The True Story of How Two Matchmakers Arranged Love in Wartime London

by
Penrose Halson

Long before the advent of modern American dating services, two 24-year-old English women, Heather Jenner and Mary Oliver, joined efforts in 1938 to assist both single men and women in finding suitable marriage partners. It was a novel idea at the time – even ridiculed as foolish and unnecessary – but their agency, known as "The Marriage Bureau," soon became very popular, receiving hundreds of applications per day. Clients seeking their services included people from all walks-of-life, from "shopgirls to debutants, plumbers to earls, charladies to countesses," businessmen, farmers, landowners, clergymen, military men, waiters, chauffeurs, architects, doctors, postmen, manufacturers, etc. The matchmakers initially charged a small fee and collected information regarding age, background, social class, work, hobbies, interests, and personal preferences regarding height, weight, hair color, and personality traits. If they succeeded in bringing together two people who "hit it off," a larger fee would be expected upon the marriage. Both women were very professional, recording all necessary data and filing it accordingly. Some of the letters they received from prospective spouses make amusing reading:

A South African gentleman farmer required "Good old family, good health, good rosy colour, auburn hair, not moon-faced, not bandy-legged, in fact good to look at. Not prudish. Not subject to mooch. Must be prepared to live in So. Africa. Must have 800 pounds unearned, free of tax. Ought to be mainly self-supporting after my decease."

A certain Sheikh enumerated his requirements: "She must be a smart lady who would entertain his guests in style. She must be charming and sophisticated, English, elegant, slim and beautifully dressed by couturiers. Not clothes off the peg, *no Never!* Without children, not a day over 45 and not an inch over 5'3." Well-born. Aristocratic with a knowledge of the world and its ways and an excellent income to match my own."

Some meetings turned into marital bliss as with Ada Burns sending a message upon her upcoming marriage to John Parker: "Dear Miss Oliver, John Parker and I are suited. Thank you. Yours faithfully. Ada Burns but soon to be Mrs."

Some patrons were eager to talk about sex which Mary found much more difficult than Heather who had attended a boarding school as a child and was familiar with farming families, as well as breeding horses and hounds. When one of the male callers mentioned to their secretary that he "was keen on fellatio," she replied "That's stamp collecting, isn't it? Yes, I am sure we can help you!"

The agency survived and even flourished during the London Blitzkrieg. They gained a reputation as being honest and reliable and both women became adept, developing a sort of sixth sense, at recognizing fortune-hunters of either sex. One give-away was when a female had no concern about marrying a much-older man, probably anticipating early widowhood and a great inheritance. As for male clients, many were especially self-conscious about baldness. As for the women, few wanted to meet a baldie. One stipulated, "No fat men, bald men, redheads, Welshmen, or parsons." Another, however, was "happy to be introduced to any man, fat or thin, short or tall, hair or no hair, provided he was a wealthy gentleman who will help me realize my ambitions. I do not want to be a domestic drudge."

Heather went on to write an advice column in the *Metropolitan Times* somewhat like a later American newspaperwoman Ann Landers. Many of the letters came from servicemen or their wives separated by war from their spouses for years who found solace in the arms of others. Eventually in 1953, she wrote a book *Marriage Is My Business* in which she described her common- sense approach in dealing with the wild aspirations of those seeking a wife. For example, one young man wanted to "meet a girl who looked like and dressed like Betty Grable right down to the little raffia skirt she had worn in her latest film." Heather pointed out that as he was an office clerk with a salary of 600 pounds a year, such a girl "might not fit into his life." Eventually he decided that this ideal might be farfetched.

This book about two women, whose mission in life was getting people married, provides interesting reading, particularly in defining the motivations that drive various people to seek a mate. In this sense, it is a sort of study in psychology. Heather, in particular, was grateful to find that she had a calling for this work and regarded matchmaking as a job and profession to which she was very well suited.

The supplement at the back may be the most intriguing part of this book as it lists the requirements of female clients between 1939-49. There are MANY. To list only a few, one woman wanted a partner who is "not amorous" … Another -- "above all, a man who will talk to me"; A third… "someone born in February or May" … Others, "I don't mind how ugly" … "someone who has known loneliness" … "no one with false teeth" … "a man who was disabled through war injuries and needs some care and help." These enumerated desires regarding a husband are extremely revealing of the characters and needs of the women who specified them and give the reader much to ponder regarding what is essential and desirous in a good marriage.

SUPPLEMENT: FOR AND ABOUT KIDS

GREAT BOOKS FOR KIDS

Not all books appeal to all children. I found that out only too soon in teaching. The key is to find some that appeal to their imagination. The books carefully chosen on the following pages not only develop interesting plots and portray intriguing characters, but also reinforce qualities we hope to inculcate: courage, empathy, perseverance, responsibility, a sense of right and wrong, a sense of compassion, an understanding of the human condition, an appreciation of a high-quality book and what makes it truly outstanding. So many of the works recommended here accomplish just that. *Counting on Grace* by Newberry Medal winner Elizabeth Winthrop, *The War That Saved My Life* by Kimberly Brubaker Bradley, *The Hired Girl* by Laura Amy, *The Christmas Sweater* by Glenn Beck, and my favorite of all, *Wonder* by R. J. Palacio are extremely effective in developing these very desirable attributes. In addition, books like *The Boy in the Striped Pajamas* and *The Boy at the Top of the Mountain,* both by John Boyne and both extremely heart-rending tales about innocent children caught up in the Holocaust, provide not only a sense of history at that time, but also provoke consideration of prejudice, persecution, and injustice. These two, however, are suitable for older, more mature kids who can handle this subject matter. Truly delightful for the younger child are the animal characters in *Tales of Zolftic, Appleblossom the Possum,* and *Flora* and *Ulysses*, all of which tell entertaining stories while offering great vocabulary which I have listed with each story. *Friday Barnes: Girl Detective* and *Women in Science: 50 Fearless Pioneers Who Changed the World* are both aimed at intelligent, clever, bright, spirited, and ambitious young girls who want to be action-oriented. The first is fun while the second encourages aspiration to leave one's mark by contributing to society and the world at large.

Following these are books about children, parenting, and raising kids. I am only too willing to offer them to you hoping that they will benefit you and your children.

Donna DeLeo Bruno

AGES 4-8

Appleblossom the Possum

Flora and Ulysses

Tales of Zolftic

AGES 9-10

When Mischief Came to Town

Roller Girl

The Land Without Color

Circus Mirandus

AGES 11-14

Wonder

Al Capone Does My Shirts

Counting on Grace

The War That Saved My Life

The Hired Girl

Fish in a Tree

Friday Barnes: Girl Detective

Booked

The Christmas Sweater

Books that Transport to Other Places

AGES 12-16

Women in Science: 50 Fearless Pioneers Who Changed the World

The Boy in the Striped Pajamas (to be found in first section)

The Boy at the Top of the Mountain (to be found in first section)

AGES 15-18

Everything, Everything

Waiting for June

Another Brooklyn

The Absolute Diary of a Part-time Indian

ABOUT KIDS, PARENTING, and EDUCATION

Grit: The Power of Passion and Perseverance

Quiet: The Power of Introverts in a World That Can't Stop Talking

Where You Go Is Not Who You'll Be

How Children Succeed: Grit, Curiosity, and the Hidden Power of Character

How to Teach Your Children Shakespeare

APPLEBLOSSOM THE POSSUM

by
Holly Goldberg Sloan

This is one endearing story about a unique theatrical family of marsupials who are given to quoting Shakespeare; for them, "All the world's a stage." Since possums are nocturnal, most of their adventures occur at night; and since they are nomadic, their Mama encourages them early on to go out on their own to seek independence. First, she teaches them life-skills for possums, such as avoiding "dangerous creatures who walk on two legs and watch boxes with light and sounds all day." Also dangerous are "metal monsters" called cars and trucks that "can flatten an animal in an instant!" And the "hairies" who bark and growl are the scariest, furriest, and most highly "unpredictable." Of course, after all these admonitions, Amlet and Angie and Alberta and Alphonse and Antonio and Alejandro as well as the youngest, Appleblossom, hook tails in shared trepidation (illustrations are adorable). But Mama reminds them that they are fast, intelligent, and clever and possess a very strong asset -- their "stink gas," a useful weapon when cornered. And so their adventures begin. Their antics will delight children, particularly 4 - 9 year-olds, who will see that fear of new experiences can be overcome. In fact, when Appleblossom accidentally falls down a chimney and actually encounters the two-legged "monsters," she will become fast friends with one -- a lonely little girl who lives in the house. There are many lessons to be learned here, especially from the very wise Mama possum who tells them "Never be afraid to make a fool of yourself by asking questions" and Antonio, when venturing out into the world for the first time, repeats her words "Love all, trust a few, do wrong to no one." The best advice, in my opinion, occurs as the brother and sister possums hesitate to go to the aid of Appleblossom -- one of the siblings reminds the others that "The most important thing in the world is family. That's why we are going to help our sister." These are charming, well-rendered characters whose comments made me chuckle. For example, Poppa Possum tells them in a serious tone, "The secret to a good relationship is to listen to your wife and agree with her whenever possible."

Portions of the dialogue are also quite amusing for adults who might choose to read it to younger children. Antonio tells his dad that Mama is "progressive"; she encouraged each of them to choose their own name. And since possums live independently on their own, as do Poppa and Mama, they need to tell him what they have learned from Mama.

"So she's progressive is she?" he replies to Antonio. " What's that make you, little critter? The brainy baby."

Antonio is quick to answer. "We don't believe in labels. Or bullying."

In this indirect manner, the author is conveying beneficial information to children while simultaneously entertaining them.

There are two additional features to this book which I loved. First, since I am a lover of Shakespeare and believe kids should be exposed to him as early as possible, this book accomplishes that. When Appleblossom senses a dog approaching, she thinks, "By the pricking of my thumbs, Something wicked this way comes" (from *Macbeth,* Act I) and at the story's end: "All's well that ends well" (title of play by Shakespeare).

In addition to familiarity with lines from "The Bard" are the author's inclusion of great vocabulary words. I do not suggest that they be presented to the child as a list to be learned, but incorporated in discussion of the story between parent and child. If the child is able to read it himself/herself, he/she would gain practice figuring out their meaning through context clues.

marsupial	nocturnal	consoling	maestro
alliance	slumbering	distracted	inventory
camouflage	savor	unpredictable	bellow
no vacancy	mutter	barely perceptible	disdain
grooming	anticipation	reassure	cavorting
banished	rejoices	permanent	crooner
progress	enhance	troupe	research
precariously	stagnant	lunge	

FLORA & ULYSSES

by
Kate DiCamillo

Flora & Ulysses is a witty, amusing tale with whacky and quirky characters. First, we have 11-year-old Flora Belle Buckman and her magical friend Ulysses, a squirrel who, in the first chapter, is accidentally sucked up into Flora's mother's vacuum cleaner. This necessitates Flora giving him CPR, much to Mrs. Buckman's dismay; she thinks he is a disgusting and rabid creature. Some of the events, as this one, are illustrated in very cute cartoons which tickle the funny bone; one illustrates Ulysses tangled in the highly teased, upswept hair-do of their neighbor Rita. Flora's mother is intent on "getting rid" of Flora's pet in the most permanent manner; but Flora's dad and a new sort- of-weird friend, a young boy William Shiver, come to the rescue. Another reason Mrs. Buchman finds Ulysses irritating is that the squirrel uses her typewriter to compose poems; the typewriter is "off limits" to everyone since she is an author of romance novels which Flora, a declared "cynic," finds ridiculous, especially because her mother is divorced from her husband. In addition to following Flora's and Ulysses' delightful adventures, youngsters will benefit from the vocabulary DiCamillo employs telling the tale. On the following page is a list that might help the young reader to understand in advance so that these unfamiliar words do not interfere with a smooth reading of the story; or, better yet, while actually reading, the child may gain more benefit from using context clues to determine the meaning. Do not be intimidated by vocabulary; the words below are used to tell a "fun" story.

coherence   fraught   prevail   speculate
capacious   obfuscate   inanimate   loathe
retract   perpetual   eons   appellation
illusion   euphemism   reside   advent
illuminated   conjured up   navigate   manifestation
banished   inconsequential   notorious   insomnia
documented   relentless   vanquish   provoke
fray

TALES OF ZOFTIC

by
Andrea Macvicar

The main character of this charming book is Zoftic, a lovable Labrador totally devoted to her Master -- "how much she cared to see him smile, to see his eyes light up awhile." The rhyme and iambic rhythm which is maintained throughout the story will be very appealing to children who delight in sound, particularly alliteration and assonance which are also used to great effect: Zoftic's friend Zeke is "a Doxie with a lot of moxie" whose plight is both "desperate and dire." Macvicar, the author, creates many amusing images which a child can easily visualize, as when Zoftic, plunged in bath bubbles, "slippery body sliding round" causes his Master to smile by "licking the suds upon his nose, upon his hair, his cheeks, his clothes." Such delight in pets is something that will resonate with kids, as will Zoftic's anxiety when his Master brings home a woman he is planning to marry: "Jealousy rules heart and head; A woman in my Master's bed!" A child can easily relate to this fear of being displaced by the arrival of a new family member, usually a baby. Moreover, kids like repetition and the author uses this musical refrain at the beginning and end of chapters: "Zoftic up, Zoftic down; Zoftic all around the town." There are so many sweet moments in this book, as when Zoftic is curled up in a ball in the back seat of the car, ecstatic to be included in a honeymoon to a "romantic secret place" with Master and Helen, his new bride. And in the next chapter when Helen brings home a bundle, the canine's nose "twitches from each ebb and flow, from scents that come from down below;" and later, "Zoftic up, Zoftic down, Zoftic all around the town. Prancing happily beside, a stroller with a son inside." There are other cute episodes as when Zoftic herself falls in love with Winner, a Shepherd, and Helen spritzes Zoftic with perfume for her wedding night, following a ceremony complete with a white bridal wreath of little roses placed on Zoft's soft ears, as well as a family celebration dinner. In addition to these endearing creatures and their adventures, this book also provides a means for a child to comprehend the life cycle, as both Zoftic and Winner grow old along with Master and Helen; and with their passing, life goes on. The litter of puppies that Winner sired with Zoftic is cared for by Master and Helen's little boy who has grown up to adulthood. I love the sentiment expressed at the end; "Tater Pie, the very first pick of the litter... has Zoftic's nose, and also looks very close... to Zoftic in her body shape. But there is Winner in the nape of her neck and Shepherd fur. She is the best of him and her."

This is not only a great book for reading aloud as the poetic quality of the lines becomes musical, but is also replete with new vocabulary: *murky, bliss, commiserate, jaunt, din, eject, obligation, prancing, perpetrators, enchanted, extravagance.* Your child will love this book.

Note: *Zofteg* is a German word of endearment for a female -- like "honey" or "dear." The author changed the German "teg" sound to the American English "tic" for the purposes of rhyme.

WHEN MISCHIEF CAME TO TOWN

by
Katrina Nannestad

In 1911, after the loss of her mother in Copenhagen, Denmark, Inga Maria travels alone by boat to live with her grandmother on Bornholm, an island off the Danish coast. Even though the grandmother who meets Inge at the harbor is brusque, wrinkled, and unsmiling, Inge is determined not to indulge in self-pity and keeps her tears and fears at bay. Although her new home is absent the colorful storybooks and large, squishy chairs where she delighted in curling up with her mother to read, Inge sees that this straw-thatched cottage is warm, cozy, pretty and inviting.

There is much to adapt to here in the country: first, Inge must master walking in heavy wooden clogs, as well as helping milk the cows; collecting freshly-laid eggs; mucking out the piles of poo left in the barn by the donkey Levi; feeding the pigs; carting, shoveling, and scrubbing. Although she is not used to such labor, she is glad to be distracted from her painful yearning for her mother which never abates. Inge tries very hard not to be a nuisance and maintain good manners in front of Grandmother's friends when they visit. There are elements of humor as Inge must communicate with the stubborn, braying donkey Levi; share a bedroom with a turkey named Henry; and interact with an enormous pig called Plenty, who is suckling fourteen piglets.

There are many mishaps and accidents to be sure, but Inge is relieved and delighted that her grandmother appears more amused than annoyed. In fact, when Inge begins school, which she finds strict and repressive, in desperation and boredom she speaks up, asking why girls must sit quietly on a bench at recess playing dominoes while the boys can run and play and exercise. In addition, she challenges the fact that in music class they are not allowed to dance or move to the rhythm. When she overhears a conversation between two very strange elderly sisters, friends of her grandmother, Inge discovers that her grandmother is not the harsh, stern person she initially appeared to be; but in her own youth was very feisty, fun-loving, and rambunctious. So begins a loving relationship between the two as they become close and are able to share their mutual grief and reminiscences of Inge's mother.

Another touching subplot involves am orphan boy Klaus who will temporarily become part of their little family. This is a very sweet book about surviving loss and finding love and life again in unexpected places. Moreover, it provides a good example of resilience and coping with life's adversities, even tragic ones. There are numerous references to the stories of Hans Christian Andersen, Inge's favorite author whose collection allows Inge to escape her sorrow in the creative world of his imagination. In the end, she finds that "Every man's life is a fairy tale, written by God's fingers." (Hans Christian Andersen).

ROLLER GIRL

by
Victoria Jamieson

Ten-year-old Astrid and Nicole have been best friends for as long as they can remember. It all started when bossy Rachel demanded that Astrid not touch a dead squirrel, and being an independent sort of person, Astrid defied her order. Then obnoxious Rachel started telling everyone that Astrid had rabies and should stay away from her. Nicole had been the only one to stand by her and reassure her that she was not in danger. From that day on they stuck together; that's what "BFF" (Best Friends Forever) do. But the "forever" part didn't last, much to Astrid's disappointment. Although they enjoyed doing everything together, one summer Astrid signed up for roller-skating camp and assumed Nicole would accompany her; but Nicole preferred Dance Camp and enrolled with mean girl Rachel. Suddenly Roller Skating camp didn't sound like so much fun. Kids will like the cute cartoon illustrations by the author who is a children's book designer and an avid roller-skater herself with the Rose City Rollers Roller Derby League. So she knows the game and all the falls, hard-knocks, and practice it takes to excel. In a sense this is her story of persistence and determination necessary to succeed. It is a story about being tough and not giving up, about dealing with friends who disappoint you and let you down, about getting second chances and making amends, and about sacrificing your own personal glory for the team. My 9-year-old granddaughter, an avid reader, gave this a 9.5 out of 10.

THE LAND WITHOUT COLOR

by
Benjamin Ellefson

The Land Without Color is a sort of modern-day fairy tale complete with all the elements of that genre: an evil ogre in the form of a two-headed dragon, a Goblin King with headless followers, the intimidating Crimson Guards, hissing vipers, and a Color Factory, the real enemy, which drains color from the locale. As a result, the land and its inhabitants are a drab shade of gray. Enter our protagonist Alvin who heroically embarks on a mission to rescue the kidnapped Princesses Gwendolyn and Sapphire, defeat the evil goblins who are responsible for the barren, desolate landscape, stop the damage of the Color Factory, and restore vibrancy to the village. In this attempt, he will be accompanied by Permy, a tiny squirrel, and together they will climb Shadow Mountain where both will become entangled in man-eating vines; evade the Red Guards who, although equipped with the finest armor and swords, have no brains; and avoid the King's offerings of free ice cream, doughnuts, and candy since such goodies cause lethargy. "Eating junk food fills your body with garbage, slows you down, and steals your life force," declares Alvin. As a result he consumes large amounts of string beans, broccoli, beets, asparagus, onions, and cauliflower which replenish the lost color and zest; "he was a vibrant plethora of bursting yellows, reds, and blues ... as the energy of the vegetables raced through his veins." At one point Alvin is swallowed by the dragon, but is able to escape with his trusty knife which his grandfather gave him as a gift at the beginning of the story, reminding him to keep this handy weapon with him at all times.

One educational benefit of this tale is an abundance of vocabulary words that the average child should be able to comprehend through the use of context clues: *bellowed, abyss, bounty, exhilarated, obstacle, imminent, ornate, insatiable, resonate, acknowledge, wry* -- to name just a few. Moreover, kids enjoy adventure, battles, alien creatures, princesses, chase scenes, imaginative places -- all attributes present in *The Land Without Color*. Although the author employs occasional hackneyed expressions -- "approached each other like oncoming trains ... spread out like a flock of birds ... lit up with excitement" ... the book is worthwhile in its creative development of an imaginative plot, as well as its confirmation of healthy and beneficial advice: "Eat your vegetables. Eat your vegetables" becomes the mantra of Alvin and his followers.

CIRCUS MIRANDUS

by
Cassie Beasley

Micha's grandpa Ephraim is dying and mean Great-Aunt Gertrudis has come to manage the household. Micha yearns for the days before her arrival when he and Grandpa spent hours together engaged in various fun projects like building the tree house in the backyard. Grandpa doesn't whistle anymore and spends long days in bed while Aunt Gertrudis keeps Micah away, insisting that Grandpa needs to rest. Not only is Micha forlorn about the changes she has wrought in their routine, but is also apprehensive about what the future holds. Most missed are Grandpa's stories of magic and fantasy that would hold Micah spellbound and transport both of them to an imaginary world -- one in particular he calls "Circus Mirandus." Here live the "Lightbender," a magician; and Mr. Header who runs the menagerie of uncaged animals; Strongman and Chintzy, plumed birds that carry messages; and Rosebud who concocts healing elixirs. Grandpa has made this world and its characters so real that when Micah sees Grandpa deteriorating, he is convinced that if somehow he can make contact with its inhabitants, their magic will be able to heal Grandpa. And so he sets out to do just this with the help of his best schoolmate Jenny. Jenny, an intelligent girl with a lot of common sense, does not completely "buy" all of what Micah asserts; but she knows he needs a friend at this difficult time in his life and agrees to go along. So begins their journey to "Circus Mirandus." The plot is woven successfully to keep the reader engrossed, especially when Grandpa has repeatedly mentioned that when a child, he was given a wish by the "Bender of Light" which he has chosen to reserve until absolutely necessary. Micha believes that NOW is the time to "call in" that wish and the suspense builds to see if it will save Grandpa. After all this build-up, Micha's wish is not granted in the manner in which he expected, sort of like prayers which are not always answered in the way the supplicant would hope. In fact, the conclusion leaves the reader uncertain as to what actually happens. While in the car with awful Aunt Gertrudis who is relocating him to her home in Arizona, Micha hears music -- the music of the circus beckoning him to join them. Traffic is stopped on the highway due to an earthquake so Micah is able to run from the car toward the sounds of drums and pipes, jumping over a chasm leaving Aunt Gertrudis and the other onlookers behind. "The Lightbender spreads his arms wide to receive him: How do you like my miracle?" Personally, I did NOT like the "miracle" which is subject to a number of interpretations. The last sentence reads, "You never need an invitation to go home." Although *Circus Mirandus* is currently popular, appearing on "Best-seller" lists for children, some aspects bother me. The focus on magic is one, particularly in this grave situation; the conclusion where Micah, trusting in the magical "Light-bender," hurls himself across the abyss is another. Moreover, the theme of escape from problems does not "sit well" with me. As a reviewer, I am like a "deliverer of the message," making readers aware of what books are garnering both attention and acclaim. In this case, I didn't much like the "message."

WONDER

by
R. J. Palacio

Wonder is one superb book for kids (primarily ages 8-15) which I enjoyed immensely myself. For a debut novel, it is remarkable. The main character Auggie is a ten-year-old with a genetically caused extreme facial deformity. Because his grossly misshapen appearance causes stares and discomfit, his parents have decided that he be home-schooled by his mother. The family includes his older sister Olivia ("Via") who is very protective and loves him dearly. Nevertheless, she sometimes resents that her brother has been the center of attention since his birth and the twenty-three surgeries he has had to undergo in his young life. This story is beautifully layered with portions that are so eloquent and heart-breaking. First, it centers on the parents' decision to have Auggie attend school for fifth grade which is where the book begins. Of course, he is reluctant -- not knowing what to expect, unfamiliar with an academic setting, anticipating ridicule and ostracism because of his looks, which does occur. Nevertheless, he summons his courage, and with the help of new schoolmates, Summer and Charlotte, as well as his understanding and devoted family, he is able to make progress. It is not an easy trek; your heart aches for the taunting and cruel remarks he must endure at the mercy of mean classmates. But you come to respect his resilience and immense desire to experience new things. There are so many scenes in which the reader will cry with and for Auggie: the one at the school Halloween party where, disguised under his costume, he overhears his best friend Jack laughing along with others who refer to him as "Freak," "Mutant," "Monster," "Zombie Kid," "E.T.," "Lizard Face," "Rat Boy," and "Freddy Krueger." Devastated by this betrayal, he flees, sobbing uncontrollably, so hurt by the one classmate who seemed able to accept him for who he was. In the opening chapter, Auggie warns the reader, "I won't describe what I look like. Whatever you're thinking, it's probably worse," and indeed it is. Because of this setback, he vows never to return to school, where others refuse to sit next to him in class and cafeteria, and run to wash their hands after touching the same pencil -- cruelly joking that they will catch the "plague." Retreating to the haven of his room, he cries, "Mommy, why do I have to be so ugly?"; and her sorrow and love for him are almost palpable when she reassures him that "he is beautiful -- a wonder." Another layer the author develops involves his sister's feelings of neglect and loss having been repeatedly eclipsed by the needier sibling, and the guilt she experiences regarding her jealousy.

Through all Auggie's trials and tribulations, -- and they are many -- the reader roots for him, laments with him, and hopes with him. You ache to embrace this wonderful, lovable boy. One of the author's greatest talents is her ability to capture the true voices of kids, and another is her sensitive treatment of this broken child. The family dynamics are also revealed in the very loving hugs, kisses, encouragement, unconditional acceptance and support of his parents and sister, who honestly see him as "an ordinary kid (although with an extraordinary face)." He is their treasured child, no matter what. There are lessons for a child to learn here: that ALL are worthy of our respect and compassion; that determination and persistence can help one overcome obstacles; that although today might be awful, tomorrow may be better; and that sometimes, despite how difficult it is, one needs to take a risk, despite the fear and pain. The reader is so drawn into Auggie's mind that it is impossible not to feel compassion for his burden. In this way, it manages to teach empathy for the less fortunate. Auggie's keen intelligence, courage, sweetness, and sense of humor will impress upon the young reader that it's what is on the inside of an individual that is of the utmost significance, not the exterior. I have seldom read a more moving book -- humanity at its best!

AL CAPONE DOES MY SHIRTS

by
Gennifer Choldenko

It is 1935 on the island of Alcatraz where the Flanagan family, comprised of Mom, Dad, 12-year-old Moose and his older, autistic sister Natalie, reside near the famous prison where Dad works as an electrician. It is an unusual place to grow up, near a building that houses some of the most notorious criminals of that time, including the Chicago gangster Al Capone, whose first assignment there was in the laundry room. This is one great book for kids 11-15, as well as those with autistic siblings. Moose has the ultimate responsibility of caring for Natalie since both Mom and Dad need to work to support the family, and his constant attachment to his sister makes for an ambivalent relationship. Moose is the one who is most adept at handling her unpredictable behavior, but it severely limits his play and interaction with his friends. Of course, there are enterprising kids on Alcatraz who want to capitalize on their proximity to the infamous gangster and devise a profitable scheme whereby they charge a nickel for each item of clothing they collect from their classmates to have laundered in the prison, supposedly by Capone. Choldenko creates an interesting cast of characters, including the intimidating warden; his scheming, mischievous daughter Piper; as well as other kids who are obsessed with anything related to Capone. Their antics are entertaining, but the heart of the story focuses on Moose's closeness to Natalie and the multitude of emotions with which he struggles daily: deep affection, resentment, frustration, anger, protectiveness. The author allows the reader to get into his head and heart; and those with such a sibling can well relate to his negative feelings toward his mother who focuses all of her attention on the needier sister. I, as well as my 12-year-old grandson, couldn't put it down. This is one OUTSTANDING kids' book not to be missed.

COUNTING ON GRACE

by
Elizabeth Winthrop

A book of historical fiction, *Counting on Grace* is a book for middle-school students. Set in 1910 in North Pownal, Vermont, it traces the sorry existence of workers in textile mills, which included very young children. One of them was Addie Card on whom the author bases her main character Grace Fourcier, a feisty, independent, and proud 11-year-old from a French-Canadian family. Both her parents and sister are employed in the local mill, although her father has been let go temporarily. Dexterity, adroitness, nimble hands, and stamina are required to keep the spindles and gears operating non-stop. Money is very tight and they are forever in debt for overdue rent as well as food purchased from the local company store, also run by the owner of the factory, Mr. Depree who exploits and cheats them whenever possible. But Grace is a bright girl who, before she is summoned to work at the mill, manages to get some education from her kind and dedicated schoolteacher Ms. Lesley. Since she is able to read, write, and calculate, she confronts Mr. Dupree about his dishonesty. Work in the mills is tedious, dirty, and dangerous since the hair, clothing, or arm of the looms' operators can easily become caught in the machinery, which is what happens to Grace on one occasion. Tangled in the machinery, nearly crushed in its jaws, Grace vows never to return. A similar accident befalls her best friend Arthur, a brilliant student, who dreams of escaping his sad and hopeless predicament to study law. Broken and desperate, unable to bear even one more day of drudgery and despair, he deliberately feeds his hand into a machine so that he will be incapacitated to continue working there and be able to return to school. This is a powerful and poignant story about the deplorable working conditions rampant in these workhouses and the children whose lives and health were sacrificed for profit. Grace and her co-workers chronically suffer respiratory ailments, constantly coughing up globs of greasy cotton balls, lint particles flying everywhere in the air around them, clogging their nasal passages and lungs. Sometimes she feels that she cannot breathe nor swallow, a common result of such working environments. But working to change all this is their beloved teacher, Ms. Lesley, who refuses to condemn them to a lifetime of toil. Read to find out how she plans a rescue from this despicable and hopeless hellhole that is all they know. For this purpose, she will seek the aid of Lewis Hine, an actual advocate for enforcement of laws prohibiting the abuse of children as cheap labor. It was his heart-rending and graphic photographs which highlighted the plight of these malnourished and overworked kids -- one as young as 7 carrying bins larger and heavier than himself, for up to 12 hours a day.

    This is my first encounter with Elizabeth Winthrop who has not only penned sixty books but who was also awarded the Newberry Medal for *Out of the Dust,* which I am now eager to read. In *Counting on Grace*, Winthrop creates a character who inspires your admiration for her spunk, work ethic, and devotion to her family, especially her beloved grandfather Pepe. The author evokes the reader's sympathy for this poor, forlorn child and her counterparts, like Arthur, whose dreams for an education and a better life seem impossible. You lament their condition, empathize with them, cheer them on. Another of Ms. Winthrop's talents is the ability to generate a clear sense of place, to recreate the dour mill towns and bleak factories where these children sacrificed their youth and health. She is most adept at this and has written a compelling tale about a sad period in our country.

THE WAR THAT SAVED MY LIFE

by
Kimberly Brubaker Bradley

A sweet and touching story, *The War That Saved My Life,* is set in England during WW II and focuses on two children, Ada and her younger brother Jamie, living with their abusive mother in London at the beginning of WWII. In addition to being neglected and underfed, housed in a filthy one-room flat, Ada, because of her club-foot, is perpetually rejected by her mother who keeps her hidden indoors and, for punishment, confines her daughter to a cramped cabinet beneath the kitchen sink. Ada's deformity is repulsive to her mother who has convinced Ada that she is unlovable and uneducable. Ada and Jamie's reprieve comes when children are being evacuated from the city into the English countryside where they might be safer from the impending blitz (bombing) of London by the Germans. Here in a picturesque, salubrious farming village, they are placed in the care of Susan Smith, an educated single lady who is grieving the loss of her best friend and house-mate Becky. Susan insists that she knows nothing about raising children and is ill-equipped for the responsibility, but the government agent in charge of relocation shames her into taking them in. Ada is the more difficult of the two children since she is struggling with so many conflicting emotions: constant pain from her badly scarred foot which bleeds, scabs, and has never been properly treated; anger and hurt from her mother's cruelty; shock at all that she has never been exposed to (she doesn't even know how to use utensils or toilet facilities, nor how to read and write). She is uncomfortable accepting Susan's kindness, confused about how to respond. She is even puzzled about the purpose of a table-cloth or curtains, all of which are unfamiliar to her since she has never seen these most common things. Fearful of closeness and touch -- all that she is used to are beatings -- she remains very guarded and distrustful despite all of Susan's efforts to reassure her. Nagging in her sub-conscious is the certainty that all this will disappear when she and her brother must certainly return to their mother in London. Most healing for Ada is "Butter," the frisky colt that once belonged to Becky. Once the caretaker of a nearby property designs a suitable saddle for her disability, Ada has never known such freedom and independence riding across the green and gorgeous landscape, bursting with flowers and natural beauty. Very slowly the still resistant Ada begins to heal. For the first time they celebrate a Christmas, complete with a Christmas feast, decorated fresh tree, gifts and carols. Another first is the celebration of their birthdays, dates which Susan must make up for them since their mother has never ever acknowledged their existence. I cannot exaggerate the meanness of this despicable mother, worse than those depicted in fairy tales like "Hansel and Gretel" or " Cinderella." And although Susan did not initially "want" them, which Ada brings up at every opportunity she can, both children thrive in her care and nurturing. Wise and aware of Ada's deep scars, both physical and emotional, Susan exercises extreme patience with this badly damaged child's outbursts and unexplained crying fits. When she reaches out to Ada who withdraws, expecting a slap or blow, Susan does not push her and allows her space. Only when Ada is flailing against Susan, as when they must descend for safety into the underground bunker which reminds Ada of the imprisonment in her mother's cupboard, does Susan wrap her arms around the girl, holding her tight until the child's energy is expended. At the end, Susan is also intent on arranging surgery to correct Ada's deformity, something her own mother had deliberately disregarded. This is an excellent story of mistrust that turns into love, of cruelty that is replaced with kindness and caring, of healing from intense abuse to confidence and realization of self-worth. Moreover, it smoothly weaves the narrative with the history of Great Britain during a tumultuous war, one which parallels the internal war being waged within this girl's psyche. This book is intended for young adults, but it is certainly worthwhile for adults as well -- an excellent story that I immensely enjoyed.

THE HIRED GIRL

by
Laura Amy

What a refreshing book and charming protagonist! *The Hired Girl* refers to 14-year-old Joan Skraggs who, after the death of her beloved mother, flees her loveless home ruled by a tyrannical and emotionally abusive father. She is found on the streets of Baltimore by a kind young man who brings her home to his Jewish family, the Rosenbachs, where she becomes the "hired girl." In this cultured and elegant home, her real life will begin, despite the fact that she is merely a domestic. First, she will have access to the family library teeming with the classics which will inspire her in her most sincere ambition to become a "noble and refined person with only lofty thoughts."

Embarrassed by her extremely hard-scrabble beginnings, limited education, and lack of class, she is so earnestly bent on self-improvement that often her efforts are so over-the-top as to become amusing. She so yearns for "dignity, sophistication, and poise"; to know how to use a "well-turned phrase"; to forego "giddy pleasures," so that she will no longer be an ignorant farm girl. The many books she obtains in the Rosenbach library will enable her to better express herself by using phrases she encounters in her readings; she recalls that beauty can "ennoble and edify" and she so wants that for herself; she "aches with indignation" and sometimes "feels affronted" or "abashed"; she begins to refer to the city as an "imposing metropolis"; her heart is often "o'ercharged and seems to swell"; a "rapturous tempest stirs in her bosom"; she feels the need to be more "formally attired" but then remorsefully chastises herself for "accursed vanity." (I just love the quaint phrasing!) She begins to model herself after heroines she admires in novels: Jane Eyre (by Charlotte Bronte) and Florence Dombey (from Charles Dickens) so as to emulate their "courage and resolution." She is enthralled and enchanted by everything to which she is exposed -- opera, art, architecture and fashion -- so much so that her innocence and naiveté are endearing. Even her hesitation to mention "indelicate subjects," such as changing the bed sheets or asking directions to the ladies' room, are amusing.

    A 2015 Newberry Award Winner, *The Hired Girl* is an excellent choice for young readers as well as adults, since it is a "coming of age" tale told in diary format which provides insight into the heart of the main character as she vacillates between elation and despair, depending upon her daily experiences. In addition, for the art-enthusiast, each of the seven sections of the book is introduced by a classical painting or engraving aptly chosen for the contents of that particular chapter: "Girl Reading" (Winslow Homer), "The Warrior Goddess of Wisdom" (Michelangelo), "The Maidservant" (W. A. Breakspeare), "Mariana in the Moated Grange" (J.E. Millais). etc. This is one girl's delightful odyssey -- complete with romance and enlightenment, hope and aspiration that ends with her typically melodramatic line: "Tomorrow, oh tomorrow! What will me destiny be?" I loved this book and recommend it highly.

FISH IN A TREE

by
Lynda Mullaly Hunt

This is a book for kids who feel like "outsiders" for any number of reasons. Ally, the main character, feels "stupid" because she has never been able to read despite advancement to the sixth grade. In every school she has attended, her dyslexia has remained undiagnosed causing her humiliation and self-consciousness. As a defense against pain and lack of confidence, she resorts to wise-cracks and clever retorts to classmates who ridicule her. Also hurting and rejected by the "in crowd" is the "nerdy," heavy-set, but brilliant Albert, a scientific master-mind who is always hungry for both food and knowledge. The child of a single mother living in poverty, he shields himself from both physical and emotional abuse by taking "the higher road" refusing to dole out violence in return for the bullying and beatings he receives. Both Allie and Keisha, another sixth grader who is ostracized for her race, recognize Albert's super-intelligence and urge him to fight back. All three are considered misfits and teased mercilessly by a group of "mean-girls" led by the detestable and insulting snob Shay and her cohorts. Heading this class is a new teacher, Mr. Daniels, who addresses them on the first day of school as his "Fantasticos." Lest you dismiss this as a mediocre book relying on stereotyped characters and a plot based on the pat, overworked formula of the enlightened teacher changing all their lives, it is much more than that. As Mr. Daniels patiently and painstakingly develops a rapport with Ally, who initially offers only resistance in return, he recognizes that beneath this hard exterior is a quick mind as well as artistic talent. It is through the game of chess that he wins her trust and develops her self-esteem. His choice of chess is significant because dyslexics "learn in pictures" which often makes them good chess players. He also explains that people learn in different ways and uses excellent analogies that kids will easily understand. For example, he asks her, "When you ride your bike home, are there different ways for you to get there? ...Well, there are also different ways for information to reach the brain and some students have trouble learning words with just their eyes." As a result, he incorporates her other senses to practice letters and sounds, even having her practice writing them in shaving cream and pink and blue sand. All is not smooth sailing, as for each step forward there are two steps backward; and Ally is faced with what she once perceived as the impossible task of achieving literacy. Regarding reading, the author Lynda Hunt does a masterful job having Ally explain to Mr. Daniels how she experiences with extreme trepidation the written page on which the letters seem to move and wiggle and appear backwards. More of Ally's description of how she experiences her disability will definitely resonate with kids facing the same challenge. Moreover, such students will be enlightened as well as reassured by Mr. Daniels' very understandable explanations of how some kids are "wired" differently which does not mean that they are deficient in any way. Another excellent book on this learning disability is Patricia Polacco's *Thank You, Mr. Faulkner*, but it is for a much younger child. Speaking of Patricia Polacco, who despite struggling with dyslexia as a child became an author, Mr. Daniels mentions her when he introduces a game to the class asking them to identify pictures of famous people and their contributions. As they identify Alexander Graham Bell, George Washington, Henry Ford, Albert Einstein, Pablo Picasso, Whoopi Goldberg, Muhammed Ali, John Kennedy, Winston Churchill, John Lennon, and Walt Disney among others, he informs them that these greatly accomplished people all struggled with simple words; and based on this and other clues, most experts believe that they all had dyslexia. I can't think of a more encouraging fact for both students and parents. I also loved the ending which is echoed in the title: "Things are going to be different. It's like birds can swim and fish can fly. *Impossible to possible*...And remember: Great minds don't think alike." What a positive message!!!

FRIDAY BARNES
Girl Detective
by
R. A. Spratt

Friday Barnes is indeed one astute, clever, witty, observant 11-year-old. Since she is the youngest child whose birth was a surprise to her parents both fully absorbed in their individual careers, she is left to fend for herself. Friday is a bit unusual in her dress and in her interests so she does not attract many friends. As a result, she spends a lot of time alone reading detective stories and poking around. Her sleuthing is encouraged by her Uncle Bernie, an ex-cop who now works for an insurance company as an investigator. Each Thursday night when he "babysits" Friday, he hashes over with her his latest assignment and usually she is of immense help in figuring out a case. In one instance, she earns a $50,000 reward from an insurance company in discovering the culprit in a bank theft. With this hefty sum, she chooses to enroll in an elite boarding school which poses new challenges, like fitting in and being accepted. Unconventional and perpetually curious, Friday is often in trouble with the headmaster who finds her intuitiveness unsettling, especially when she seems to deduce much about his own behavior and personality. However, when she begins to use her skills to unearth the cause of some mysterious occurrences at the school, the headmaster must give Friday her due.

Kids, particularly girls ages 10-14, will find this smart, no-nonsense girl very appealing and admirable for her analytical mind. The mysteries she solves -- disappearing homework, stolen desserts, a mysterious swamp creature -- all comprise an engaging story as she moves from solving one mystery to another.

Friday is a modern-day Nancy Drew who thoroughly entertained me when I was an upper-elementary student. She might also be considered the female equivalent of Encyclopedia Brown, the main character in another such series very popular with my own sons. I expect that this current series, beginning with this first book and continuing with *Friday Barnes: Under Suspicion*, will bring hours of entertainment to kids looking for wholesome, pleasurable reading. In addition, Spratt, the author, incorporates great vocabulary words for kids to easily master through context clues: *harass, intimidate, smolder, voluminous, smug, assumption, assessment, allegation, diversion, redundant, malfunction, heinous, fastidious, infuriate, chivalrously, preferable, impressive, intonation, subsequent, glum* -- to name just a few. The "educator" in me would encourage mid-upper elementary teachers to use this book as an excellent choice of reading and vocabulary material for their students. In fact, it could also serve as a worthwhile lesson in legal fairness: the necessity of open-mindedness free of preconceived opinions, avoiding assumptions before proper evidence is gathered, the methodical step-by-step analysis such as Friday follows. Finally, this book has much material around which a skillful teacher could build myriad worthwhile lessons.

BOOKED

by
Kwame Alexander

A recipient of the Newberry Medal as well as other awards for his previous book *The Crossover*, Kwame Alexander has used an unusual layout for this tale told entirely in free verse -- a poetic form which ignores rhythm, rhyme, and punctuation. The main character Nick relays his own story in words scattered vertically down each page as chapters in his life: boring English class, weird teachers, senseless homework assignments, his favorite sport soccer, his best friend Cobey, trouble in school with bullies, his crush on a classmate named April -- all issues to which kids can relate. Most of his thoughts and feelings, however, focus on the impending divorce of his parents which causes him pain, sadness, and conflict. Angry, unsettled, and resentful, Nick hopes that somehow they will reconcile and that stability and security will return to his home. Throughout all these experiences, Nick is learning to deal with life's disappointments and challenges. Many of the chapters are presented as "conversations" -- with his mom, his dad, his best friend, his teacher, the school librarian, the principal, his nemeses the twins Dean and Don, a family therapist when his parents are concerned about how poorly he is taking their separation -- and the dialogue in each rings true to kids of that age. In addition to a story whose subject matter will resonate with kids ages 9-15, is the added benefit of exposure to new and unusual vocabulary words. Since his dad is the author of a dictionary, he insists that Nick gradually master all the words defined within its pages: examples are *farrow, flummoxed, logorrhea, codswallop, cachinnate, pugilism, malapropism, rapprochement*, etc. I recommend this unusual and clever "novel-in-verse" which deals with adolescent problems such as coping with shattering news, adjusting to life's vicissitudes, finding courage to stand up to bullies, as well as directly and honestly approaching the opposite sex.

THE CHRISTMAS SWEATER

by
Glenn Beck

Based on a true story, *The Christmas Sweater,* by TV and radio host Glenn Beck, deserves to become a holiday classic. 12-year-old Eddie is eagerly anticipating Christmas morning mainly because he expects to receive a very cool, red Huffy bike he has been admiring for months in the window of the local sporting goods store. He has chosen to ignore that since his father's death, life has been extremely difficult for his mom who is working four jobs just to keep them housed and fed. His misses his father terribly; but even when the family was complete, Eddie seethed with embarrassment because he lacked the basic items other kids had. One of the things Eddie considers most demeaning is that while his friends have real boots, he must cover his shoes with plastic bags from his father's bakery to keep out the ice and snow. Despite all the evidence that there is no money for extravagant gifts or toys, Eddie maintains his hope that somehow his mother will miraculously satisfy his craving for this bike which in his mind has taken on epic proportions. So, of course, when her gift for him on Christmas morning is a lovingly hand-knit sweater on which she has been working for months, Eddie is not only keenly disappointed, but enraged and angry that his life is so meager and devoid of fun. Focused on his own angst, he does not immediately see his mother's hurt; but when he does, he totally ignores it, running to his room and discarding his sweater in a heap on the floor. Eddie makes no attempt to ease his mother's pain; and when they go later to his grandparents' farm for holiday dinner and the exchange of modest gifts, he continues his sullen remarks and makes everyone miserable. What he cannot possibly know is that the red Huffy is lovingly covered and hidden in Grandpa's barn. But his behavior is so selfish and unacceptable to Grandpa, that he chooses not to indulge his beloved grandchild, particularly when he sees the tears shed by his Eddie's mother who is so overwhelmed by fatigue and worry and sadness. When Eddie demands that they cut short their visit and return home, his mother meekly protests that she is exhausted and had planned for them to spend the night at the farm. Grandpa is so distressed at Eddie's bratty behavior and disregard for his mother, that he agrees that perhaps Eddie and his Mom should head home despite the snow and frigid temperatures. He has no intention of rewarding his grandson with the dearly bought bike. So begins the next sad chapter of Eddie's life, a car accident claiming the life of his Mom, for which all will suffer heartbreak -- his grandfather, grandmother, and most of all Eddie himself.

    This is a story of forgiveness and redemption -- of an immature boy who feels cheated by life and is oblivious to the blessings around him until he nearly destroys himself and all who love him. The reader struggles with Eddie through his pain, guilt, and conflict; grieves with his grandparents for the loss of their daughter and the wayward route of their grandson as he lashes out at them, God, life, the world -- all who have let him down. It will be a long road and a long time before Eddie realizes that it is not what you are dealt that determines your life, but rather how you react to what is thrown your way. This is one poignant, dramatic story -- a sort of coming-of-age tale -- where Eddie will have to struggle through what is left of his youth to arrive at manhood with a new awareness of how to survive in life with its inherent tragedy and loss. His will be an extremely hard-earned lesson.

WOMEN IN SCIENCE
50 Fearless Pioneers Who Changed the World

by
Rachel Ignotofsky

An inspiring book for young girls keen on math, science, and technology, *Women in Science* is written for them. The author Ignotofsky's research goes far back into ancient times to trace the contributions of Hypatia, an Egyptian astronomer and mathematician; Maria Sibylla Merian (1600s), one of the greatest scientific illustrators of insects and butterflies; Mary Anning (early 1800s) who at age 11, took over her deceased father's fossil business and at age 12 discovered the first complete ichthyosaur skeleton ever found, which brings us to a dismaying fact. Anning was not allowed to publish her work because, although doctors and geologists respected her and used her findings in their own work, she was a "working class woman" who was not "even allowed to mingle with educated gentlemen." Anning was not the only woman to meet obstacles. Florence Bascom (late 1800s) who "rocked the world of geology" with her studies on how the earth's geography changes over thousands and thousands of years, had to sit behind a screen in her university courses so as not to "distract any of her male classmates." In addition, the first American doctor, Elizabeth Blackwell who graduated first in her class and earned her medical degree in 1849, faced similar discrimination. She had to sit separately from the male students because her anatomy professors were embarrassed by her presence and even asked that she leave a lecture on reproduction. She insisted on remaining even though they feared discomfort for her "feminine sensibilities." Nevertheless, these women would not allow short-sighted teachers and old-fashioned decorum to dissuade them from pursuing their interests and achieving great things. Spurred on by their persistence and love of discovery, these highly intelligent women made outstanding contributions. Among them were physicist Maria Gorppert-Mayer who won the Noble Prize in 1963 for her study of neutrons and protons; for most of her life she earned no pay. Another who worked without financial compensation for the first seven years of her career was Emmy Noether, a theoretical physicist who was an associate of the famed Albert Einstein. When she finally was given a salary, she was the lowest paid professor. Also, not given the respect she deserved, was Patricia Bath, an ophthalmologist who in 1986 invented the Laserphaco Probe to remove cataracts, restoring sight to people around the world. She was assigned an office in an undesirable location next to where the lab animals were kept. Also amazing was chemist Alice Ball, who at age 23, developed a new treatment for leprosy, a once hopeless disease; and in the late 1700s, at age 29 the great Chinese scholar Wang Zhenji published volumes on math and astrology that influenced so many who came after her. The work of these women had an impact on millions. Dr. Elizabeth Blackwell, for example, was the first to connect the spread of infection with unsanitary conditions and from her findings, we get the present day insistence on thorough hand washing in medical settings. Another was cytogeneticist Barbara McClintock, born in 1902, who "loved boxing, riding bikes, and playing baseball. She didn't fit in with girls, and the boys didn't want to play with her" -- what some would call a "misfit." She later made peers uncomfortable with her blunt, direct manner. Far ahead of them, her study led to her belief that a gene could "jump" to a different part of a chromosome and turn on and off. When Barbara gave a lecture in 1951 about this new and exciting discovery, no one believed her. She didn't take offense, stating, "When you know you're right, you don't care." Thirty years later in 1983, she was awarded the Nobel Prize.

From the stories of these fifty trailblazers, young girls can find worthy role models to emulate in every field: anthropology, astronomy, botany, engineering, pharmacology, psychology, etc. -- women from all over the world -- Italy, Iran, Germany, China, Austria, England, USA, etc.

This recent book (2016) is designed for bright, ambitious young girls who should realize that these inspiring women let nothing stop them -- not gender, nor race, nor background, nor society's opinion of "proper" roles for females. I applaud the final sentence encouraging girls to "go out and tackle problems, find answers, and learn everything you can to make your own discoveries." It's called "GIRL POWER!"

EVERYTHING, EVERYTHING

by
Nicola Yoon

The main character, 18-year-old Madeline, has never left her house. She has a rare illness, a form of "Severe Combined Immunodeficiency," commonly known as the "bubble baby disease." Allergic to the world, so to speak, she must be protected from germs, viruses, and bacteria. As a result, she needs constant monitoring of her environment. In addition, before entering the house, all visitors must be "sterilized" in an airtight, vacuum-type foyer so as not to introduce harmful agents that could kill her. But there are no visitors. She lives a sort of "solitary confinement" in a white bedroom where her mother, a physician, and a nurse Carla take her blood-pressure and temperature every hour, as well as prepare her meals. She spends her time reading, using the computer, and dreaming of what life must be like on the outside. Suddenly one day, from her bedroom window, she sees a family moving in next door and is especially attracted to a lanky, handsome boy about her age. He sees her watching him; and later that night, curious to know her better, he throws a pebble at her window. Initially she does not respond, but after repeated attempts to get her attention, she sees he has written his email address in black marker on his glass window. So begins a relationship that will change her life. Without the knowledge or permission of Madeline's mother, the nurse Carly, who is Madeline's closest confidant and friend, will allow the teen to visit for brief periods, although for Madeline's safety, he must remain at the other end of the room. Healthwise, this is very risky business; but Madeline's ardent yearning to experience life, even in such a limited manner, in addition to her pleas, convince Carly to let her take the chance. They are immediately drawn to each other, and every night, for hours, they communicate by texting. This is a most unusual story. Lest I spoil the suspense, I will only say that a romantic relationship will ensue, putting Madeline's fragile life at stake. Nevertheless, she will risk everything to be with him, if even for a short time. The author succeeds admirably at making the reader understand how a girl, with such a sheltered and cloistered life -- with no life at all -- would so crave companionship and normal teen experiences, to be eager to take the chance, regardless of the consequences. In conclusion, be prepared for an unexpected and shocking twist at the end to which the author has so cleverly been building. (Recommended for ages 15-18)

WAITING FOR JUNE

by
Joyce Sweeney

The story begins when main character Sophie, an unmarried high school senior, is in her third trimester of pregnancy. The father, whom she refuses to identify, is no longer in the picture; but she has the most supportive friend in Joshua, who is her very best ally. This tale is replete with conflict; first, between Sophie and her depressed mother who has always refused to answer her daughter's questions about her father, even his name and identity; she is also resented by Joshua's girlfriend who is jealous of their close relationship; in addition, she is finding threatening notes taped to her school locker by someone who intends her harm. This last is most puzzling because she can't imagine who this might be. As the story progresses, she experiences the typical symptoms of pregnancy, but also one that is unique -– a sort of outer-body experience resembling a dream state in which she is only aware of swimming in deep water accompanied by protective whales. In one instance, she finds herself quite far from home, in a park overlooking Biscayne Bay and needs to call Joshua to come bring her home. What she doesn't know is that the mythology surrounding whales is related to the heritage of her baby's father. This is the main mystery: who is he? And who intends to hurt her? In addition, why is Sophie's mother so secretive about Sophie's father? All this keeps the reader guessing until the end. The book is an easy and fast read. Although categorized a "teen" book, I found it quite interesting.

ANOTHER BROOKLYN

by
Jacqueline Woodson

A recipient of numerous awards, including the 2014 National Book Award, Jacqueline Woodson in this latest work, has created a lyrical and nostalgic novella about adolescent female friendship while growing up in 1970s Brooklyn. It focuses on four girls -- August (the narrator), Sylvia, Angela, and Gigi who emotionally support each other and share experiences and dreams. But the area in which they live is poverty stricken, inhabited by neglectful mothers, broken families, druggies and prostitutes, which, of course, compromises the possibility of their future aspirations. Of the group, Sylvia has the most stable home life with a family intact and a father who seems to disdain her "ghetto" girlfriends. They spend their time braiding each other's hair, listening to records, exchanging confidences, and walking the streets four-abreast, arms linked together, which seems to afford them "girl-power." Gigi has ambitions of becoming a well-known dancer and is the first to leave their neighborhood to attend a performing arts school in Manhattan. Before joining this group of girls, "Auggie" and her brother were kept under lock-and-key in their top-floor three-decker apartment by their father who feared for wayward influences on his children. But one day in utter frustration and desire for outside stimulation, her brother smashes the window and following hospitalization for his injuries, their father eases up on their confinement. Once "outside" they are exposed to teen-age temptations and all the rest that a run-down Brooklyn neighborhood has to offer. One theme that keeps recurring throughout is "Augie's" yearning for her absent mother. It permeates the entire book, both in her dreams and in her waking hours. The writing style has a poetic quality -- random thoughts interspersed with real-life events -- a stream-of-consciousness technique. Sometimes it is difficult to distinguish between reality and her dream-life.

It is not surprising that Woodson was recently named the "Young People's Poet Laureate" by the Poetry Foundation, as well as winner of the Coretta Scott King Award since her work focuses on black kids, the residents of slum neighborhoods rife with their unique challenges

THE ABSOLUTELY TRUE DIARY OF A PART-TIME INDIAN

by
Sherman Alexie

In choosing this book, I was first attracted to its uniquely creative title and the fact that it had won "The National Book Award," as well as many other honors. In addition, while thumbing through the pages, my attention was caught by its hysterical cartoons by Ellen Fornay. Although categorized as a "Young-Adult" novel, I would expect this very original tale to provide enjoyable and enlightening reading for anyone 15 years and older. The main character is Arnold Spirit , Jr., a teenage Native-American living on an Indian reservation with his family. Life is difficult with little hope of improvement; all live in poverty; many, including his dad are alcoholic, depressed, and hopeless. To add to Arnold's woes, he was born with fluid on the brain, leaving him susceptible to seizures with a skull he says is "enormous," in addition to huge arms and feet, but a pencil thin body. He says he looks "goofy" on the inside, as well as the outside. The comic strip drawings of him seem exaggerated to emphasize his feelings of "weirdness" and ostracism. However, he is extremely bright, precociously observant and wise -- traits which also contribute to his teasing and bullying by other kids. Despite his sad situation, he loves his family (mom, dad, grandmother, and sister), and feels an unspoken closeness to his best friend Rowdy who serves as his confidant and protector. But this connection drastically changes when Arnold takes the opportunity to enter a better school 20 miles away from the reservation. Rowdy feels angry since it appears to him that Arnold is severing ties to his Indian identity, as well as turning his back on his best friend. That is not the case, however. Following the loss of his beloved grandmother, the elopement of his sister with a casino poker player, and the death of his closest uncle in a drunken motorcycle mishap, Arnold begins to see that his life is likely to follow the same dead-end as all his Indian counterparts if he does not take control of his future. This change of high schools is not at all easy since sometimes his irresponsible father is too hungover to drive him to school or doesn't have enough money for gas. The dilapidated car is often unreliable and Arnold must trek the 20 miles to school. Nor does Arnold have money for lunch and often goes hungry. Most of the other students ignore or shun him since he is the only Native-American and a misfit in an all-white school of affluent kids with cars, money, and fashionable clothes. But Arnold is tough and determined and realizes soon that he is smarter than nearly every kid in the school.

This book covers a lot of ground, so to speak: the sad situation of Indians on reservations, their poverty, lack of employment, fractured culture, and prevalent alcoholism. It is also a coming-of-age story and fight to survive of one admirable boy and his struggle to bridge the social and cultural divide between the white world and life on the Indian compound. Moreover, it is told in the most enjoyable prose, in his own words, through a teen's perspective, which is sometimes so funny as to cause the reader to laugh out loud. This combination of the sad with the comic is so skillfully blended that it is a great literary achievement of the author. It is emotionally honest and heroic while simultaneously hilarious. In Arnold, Sherman Alexie has created a wonderful character with all the inner conflict and angst of a typical adolescent, but with the critical eye and precocious maturity of the successful adult he yearns to become. Arnold's story is both "tragic and tender…offbeat…heartbreaking, funny, and beautifully written." There is some profanity and a tad of sexual innuendo, which is why I recommend it for older teens. However, these elements create a tone of authenticity in dialogue used by young adults like Arnold. If anything, it enhances the reality of his persona rather than detracting in any way. THIS IS ONE GOOD BOOK! *Publishers Weekly* called it "the best book of the year" with accolades from *The New York Times, LA Times, Boston Globe, School Library Journal, Amazon.com*, and other literary periodicals.

GRIT
The Power of Passion and Perseverance

by
Angela Duckworth

Grit is the result of years of research and observation made by Angela Duckworth, a former teacher, consultant, and psychologist. For many years, she has wondered about the factors that combine to make a person successful, and in this very recent book she reveals what she has learned. Duckworth begins by focusing on new cadets at West Point Military Academy, all of whom must be high achievers to have even gained acceptance to this rigorous, grueling, and demanding institution. It is indeed a tough initiation period these boys endure in their first months of training. Even though all are mentally, physically, emotionally, and academically qualified, many will wash out in the initiation phase. Next, she focuses on salespeople who must face rejection daily and learns that 50% do not last after six months. Next, she turns her attention to "Spellbound," a national spelling competition that requires hours and hours of practice and preparation. In all instances, one's grit, defined as "dogged persistence and determination in pursuing a goal," was the most essential attribute for success, even more important than innate talent or intelligence. For, many so-called "geniuses" do not always realize their full potential if they lack the tenacity and resilience to overcome setbacks and disappointments. She uses many examples of specific individuals in all fields -- athletics, business, science, literature, politics, music, art, philosophy -- to assert that a combination of passion and determination, plus hours and hours of directed practice, combine to create "mega-successful" people. Those who have achieved the most will often tell you that they "love what they do" so that they are willing to work doggedly toward improving and reaching a goal. That one has great interest in his work is essential for peak performance. Unfortunately, worldwide only 13% of adults declare themselves "engaged" at work, so in reality very few enjoy what they do for a living. Moreover, what the author calls "paragons of grit" possess a sense of purpose, a belief that one's work is important and significant -- that it matters to others besides just himself.

Midway through the book, Duckworth offers a guide to parents, coaches, teachers, and mentors regarding how best to develop and foster "grit." In the subtle wording of their encouraging remarks, mentors can send the "right" message to urge those struggling to master a job, subject, assignment or technique. Notice the difference in the following comments:

UNDERMINES GROWTH, MINDSET, & GRIT / PROMOTES GROWTH, MINDSET, & GRIT

UNDERMINES GROWTH, MINDSET, & GRIT	PROMOTES GROWTH, MINDSET, & GRIT
"You're a natural! I love that."	"You're a learner! I love that.
"Well, at least you tired."	"That didn't work. Let's talk about how you approached it and what might work better."
"Great job! You're so talented!"	"Great job! What's one thing that could have been even better?"
"This is hard. Don't feel bad if can't do it.	"This is hard. Don't feel bad if you can't do it *yet*."

With just an adjustment of language, the mentor cultivates hope and shows he believes that the student really can achieve success with enough practice and persistence. This book provides empowering advice on how to raise a child with drive and the ability to overcome mistakes, withstand rejection, bounce back from set-backs in order to set a goal, pursue that goal, and realize great strides.

QUIET
The Power of Introverts in a World That Can't Stop Talking

by
Susan Cain

Do you prefer to listen more than talk? To while away an evening curled up with a book rather than accept an invitation to a party? Do you prefer to work on tasks alone, preferably in a closed room rather than brainstorm strategies in a group with colleagues? Are you highly empathetic to others' distress and react keenly to injustice, feel extreme emotions, deplore small talk, have a strong conscience? If so, you may be among the one-third to one-half of those often referred to as introverts. Some mothers become very concerned when their child appears shy or timid when encountering new people and new situations, or when the child's teacher notices his tendency to avoid social interaction with others. The predominant message in this book is that such a child is okay; that there is nothing wrong with these traits in and of themselves. Don't think of such "introversion" as something that needs to be cured. Some of the most successful people in the world are/were introverts: Charles Swab, Bill Gates, Brenda Barnes -- all highly effective CEOs; Albert Einstein, Mahatma Gandhi, Dale Carnegie. She asserts that today there is a bias against quiet people, that they are often mistakenly considered hermits or misanthropes since ours is an outwardly oriented society.

Extremely interesting are the many studies she cites, particularly those of Jerome Kagan, a leading Harvard researcher who studied infants' brains and behaviors at birth and whose work was picked up by his protege, Dr. Carl Schwartz at Massachusetts General Hospital using magnetic resonance imaging when these children grew up. They are the ones credited with the "high-reactive nervous system" theory. They believe that certain temperaments are innate, but also believe that environmental factors can also contribute to introversion. Their studies support the premise that introversion and extroversion are physiologically, even genetically based. Moreover, Schwartz's studies indicate that high or low reactive temperaments do not disappear in adulthood; that is, a bold or timid personality does not essentially disappear as one matures. Rather the individual can learn strategies to cope with these tendencies.

For those who undervalue the more deliberate thinking process and decision-making of "high-reactive" (introverts), remember Albert Einstein's words: "It's not that I'm so smart. It's that I stay with problems longer."

WHERE YOU GO IS NOT WHO YOU'LL BE
An Antidote to the College Admissions Mania

by
Frank Bruni

Having taught in a "Blue Ribbon" school for 35 years, I am very familiar with the angst and trepidation with which high school students approach their senior year. Many have been programmed by their parents to believe that gaining entrance into an Ivy League institution will determine their future success. In his book *Where You go Is Not Who You'll Be*, Frank Bruni, former food critic for *The New York Times,* attempts to dispel that notion. In some cases, the competition for matriculation into such an institution begins as early as kindergarten. "There is an implicit belief that a premier kindergarten program guarantees an early leg up in a nearly fourteen year battle to gain admission to the country's most competitive colleges." Further, many parents spend as much as $30,000 per year in SAT preparation, as well as tutors in multiple subject areas and mentors who oversee their child's assignments. For example, Ivy Wise, a college consulting firm, sells a "platinum package" of 24 guidance sessions, in addition to an hour of weekly phone time during junior and senior years for $30,000. All of this contributes to the hysteria regarding where a student will matriculate. What further adds to this panic is the *US News and World Report's* annual list of the top-ranking colleges in the country, contributing to a "game that's spread wildly out of control." Bruni points out that the selections are "very subjective and easily manipulated… they are more about vestigial reputations and institutional wealth… They are an attention-getting, money-making enterprise for *US News.*" Adam Weinberg, president of Denison University, says, "I think *US News and World Report* will go down as one of the most destructive things that ever happened to higher education." What was most interesting were the histories of many accomplished individuals who told their own stories of how they ended up at second or even third-tier schools and how their initial disappointment at being rejected by the Ivy Leagues turned out to be a blessing in disguise; how the so-called "lesser" schools provided them opportunities and mentors who guided them to achieve beyond anything they could have imagined.

This book is a great resource for high-school seniors considering institutions of higher learning. It helps to focus on what a school might provide you with other than a prestigious label. In addition, it gives concrete examples of people who were better off attending a "lesser" institution, proving that in the end, these venues gave them more, rather than less, of what they needed to make it.

HOW CHILDREN SUCCEED
Grit, Curiosity, and the Hidden Power of Character

by
Paul Tough

All loving parents want their children to have happy and successful lives. But how is that accomplished? In his book *How Children Succeed*, Paul Tough researches the most recent studies that try to answer that very question. Aware that the first three years are the most critical in a child's development, Tough begins by investigating the work of Michael Meaney, a neuroscientist at McGill University (Canada) whose research focuses on rats and their licking and grooming process. Results indicate that those infant pups who received the most comforting experience of licking and grooming from their mothers grew up braver, bolder, and better adjusted than those who were not so nurtured. These more fortunate babies were better at mazes, more curious, less aggressive, healthier, and lived longer lives. In humans, the closest parallel to this behavior would be attachment between mother and child. Those infants who were more securely attached became attentive, engaged, obedient in class, and able to deal with setback as students. Those whose parents were disengaged or emotionally unavailable had problems in pre-school, were anxious, anti-social, and immature. Researchers were able to predict with 77% certainty, when the child was barely 4 years old, which was likely to drop out of high school. They were even able to identify predictors, other than IQ, that were essential to a child's success: conscientiousness, extraversion, openness to experiences, grit, optimism, perseverance, and character. In nursery school the proper focus of the teacher should be to develop character rather than convey information. To develop perseverance and focus, the child also needs a high level of warmth and nurturing -- comforting, hugging, talking -- but also being allowed to fail. For example, if he falls, allow him to get up without assistance. If he makes a mistake, confront exactly how he messed up and encourage him to do better next time. Moreover, it is counter-productive for a parent to protect the child from everything or to provide him with all. A child needs discipline, rules, limits, and an occasional "No." Tough's research also shows the challenges that affluent kids face. They are more likely to demonstrate high levels of anxiety, as well as depression, because their parents are more likely to be emotionally distant while simultaneously expecting high levels of achievement. (I personally do not agree that affluent parents are more emotionally distant).

What I did find particularly intriguing is the attempt to use chess as a teaching tool to build character. Many of the later chapters are devoted to how this is done.

Character is considered of primary importance since a child may have incredible intellect, but may not know how to channel his impulses in the right direction. Character issues are defined as procrastination and social and emotional traits, such as self- control, ability to delay gratification, consideration of others, etc.

Much of the information presented in this book is a "given"; however, much is new, such as using the game of chess to teach personal skills usually left unaddressed in the higher grades where focus is on math, grammar, and language concepts.

It is replete with information about cognitive behavior therapy to counteract destructive behavior, educational strategies to model desirous behavior, new and evolving educational theory. Years ago, researcher Samuel Bowles observed that schools were rigged to create docile conformists where teachers rewarded drones for their punctuality and dependability rather than creativity, the result of which were "bland, reliable sheep." Education is changing. Much of the book's material is encouraging; for example, a mindset IS malleable. With the proper direction, pessimistic children can be redirected toward an optimistic outlook. *How Children Succeed* is not so much a handbook or primer for parents on how to raise children as it is a collection of scientific studies devoted to helping children, particularly under-privileged ones, attain their full potential.

HOW TO TEACH YOUR CHILDREN SHAKESPEARE

by
Ken Ludwig

"Oh, what a rogue and peasant slave am I."

Teach our kids Shakespeare? What a novel notion! Not only possible, asserts Ken Ludwig, the author and an acclaimed playwright, but also easy. Quoting "the Bard?"

So very preferable to other words and phrases they might pick up!!! What better first step to future entrance to an Ivy League institution? This, however, should not be your primary goal; rather both parent and children should be having fun through this interaction. He gives several step-by-step suggestions as to how to go about this.

First, break the passage into a few lines. Next, explain to the child the meaning of the line, including specific words. For example, "Look what fools these mortals be!" (from *A Midsummer Night's Dream*). Mortals are people, human beings, like you and me. Sometimes we do foolish things, make mistakes, act silly, look ridiculous. Now a child has an appropriate description of his foolish actions or those of others.

Third, memorize the line by saying it aloud, then repeating it, then saying it again, examining the rhythm; since most of the plays are written in iambic pentameter. There are so many lines suitable for use by a child in so many situations:

"I go, I go, look how I go
Swifter than an arrow from a Tartar's bow."
(Also from *A Midsummer Night's Dream*)

Of course, you would need to explain that a "tartar" is an Oriental fighter with a strong bow. What better way to convey speed which one must summon when late for school or other events?

Some others -- *"Neither a borrower, nor a lender be."*

"All that glitters is not gold."

"Parting is such sweet sorrow."
(from *Romeo and Juliet*)

"What's in a name? A rose by any other name would smell as sweet."
(also from *Romeo and Juliet*)

This is a type of "head start" different from the educational program designed for preschoolers. So ----

"Start quoting your Shakespeare

Start quoting him now;

Start quoting your Shakespeare

If you'd like your kids to wow!"

www.ingramcontent.com/pod-product-compliance
Lightning Source LLC
LaVergne TN
LVHW051826080426
835512LV00018B/2749